# Behind-the-Scenes
# BASEBALL

# Behind-the-Scenes
# BASEBALL

Real-Life Applications
of Statistical Analysis Actually Used by
Major League Teams...and Other Stories from the Inside

## Doug Decatur

Behind-the-Scenes Baseball
Real-Life Applications of Statistical Analysis
Actually Used by Major League Teams…and Other Stories from the Inside

by Doug Decatur

Edited by Andrew Yankech and John Dewan
Cover design by Tom Wright
Cover art "Behind-the-Scenes Baseball" by M.P. Wiggins, TheSpiritSource.com
Typesetting by Harvest Graphics

Copyright © 2006 Doug Decatur

Published by:   ACTA Sports
5559 W. Howard Street
Skokie, IL 60077
(800) 397-2282
info@actasports.com
www.actasports.com

Library of Congress Number: 2006920998
ISBN-10: 0-87646-300-7
ISBN-13: 978-0-87946-300-7
Printed in the United States of America
Year: 12 11 10 09 08 07 06
Printing: 10 9 8 7 6 5 4 3 2 1

# CONTENTS

Introduction • 9

Part One • 11

## Stories from One of Baseball's First Statistical Consultants

## Part Two • 49

## The GM IQ Test

## Part Three • 255

## Case Study: The Houston Astros' 2004 Run for the Pennant

## Epilogue • 305

## Acknowledgments • 311

For my sons Stephen and Joseph.
I will go outside and play baseball with you guys
as soon as I finish this one last sentence.

# INTRODUCTION

Why do I love baseball statistics? I don't. I love winning. Statistics are just a vehicle used to generate wins. Statistics can be used to find wins anywhere and everywhere. Through the use of statistics batting orders can be made more efficient, bullpen use can be made more efficient, starting lineups can be improved, the 25-man roster can be improved, in-game strategy can be improved, and more. Each and every aspect of a team can be examined and improved through the use of statistics. The result is more wins. Wins are what it is all about.

For nearly 15 years I have worked as a statistical consultant for a number of teams, including the Milwaukee Brewers, Cincinnati Reds, and Houston Astros. Another great benefit of making recommendations to a baseball team is the feeling of accomplishment you get when you see the players you recommend succeed, such as Greg Vaughn hitting 50 home runs in a season, or Brandon Backe pitching seven shutout innings in the World Series.

No, I don't love baseball statistics. I just love the results they can generate.

In 1982 I read the Bill James' *1982 Baseball Abstract* and it forever changed the way that I looked at baseball. In the Abstract, James used statistics and formulas to find the answers to tough baseball questions—everything from evaluating players to building teams. It became obvious to me that there was a gap of knowledge between Bill James and the management of major league teams. I concluded that if a major league team would just apply Bill James' findings, formulas and theories to their team, then that team would have a tremendous advantage over their competition. Today there are teams in the majors doing exactly that and they are extremely successful: the Red Sox hired Bill James in 2004 as a consultant and immediately won a World Series; the Athletics have GM Billy Beane, who uses advanced statistical methods to average 90+ wins a season despite being a small market team with a small market payroll; and the Astros have Phil Garner, the most statistically sound manager in baseball, who has led the Astros to two straight National League Championship Series and the 2005 World Series.

*Behind-the-Scenes Baseball* is written in three parts:

Part One contains stories from my early years as one of baseball's first statistical consultants. The stories are meant to give the reader a fun, inside look at baseball and a taste of what it was like working for major league teams in the nineties—both the successes and the difficulties.

Part Two is the GM IQ Test—a 100-question test on information that major league GMs and managers need to know and baseball fans want to know. This isn't a trivia test. Every question and answer can be used in some fashion by a baseball GM or manager. In 1993, while working for the Milwaukee Brewers as a statistical consultant, I began compiling the results and conclusions from important baseball research to provide the Milwaukee Brewers a statistical information advantage over the rest of the major leagues. This list was then converted into a 33-question test. Since 1993, as more research has become available, the number of test questions has grown to 100. We now have a fun test which will challenge both the average fan and baseball experts alike. The test contains questions from the best baseball research men and companies in the industry: Bill James, John Dewan, Baseball Info Solutions, STATS Inc., and the authors of *Baseball Prospectus*, to name a few.

Part Three is a case study of how Manager Phil Garner used advanced statistical information, some of the same information which is found in the test in Part Two, to overtake five teams and win the 2004 National League wild card.

Bill James led the horse to water in the 1980s with his Baseball Abstracts. In Part Three of *Behind-the-Scenes Baseball*, we not only watch that horse take a drink, we also see how it takes that drink.

# PART ONE

# STORIES FROM ONE OF BASEBALL'S FIRST STATISTICAL CONSULTANTS

Over the years many people have asked me how I became a statistical consultant for Major League Baseball teams. Well, I wrote letters and reports and more letters and reports to major league general managers telling them and showing them how the use of advanced statistical information could make a difference for their teams. Unfortunately, during the eighties baseball management really didn't pay much attention to statistics. The only people who seemed receptive were those on the verge of being fired. Thus, I would make brief connections with someone, but before any significant progress could be made, my connection would be fired or reassigned.

Then, in the winter after the 1990 season, the Milwaukee Brewers answered one of my letters and requested a sample report. I completed the report and sent it off. A couple of weeks later, the fantasy league I was in had its draft. I drafted an obscure Brewers pitcher in the last round. One of the guys in the league knew I was hoping to hear from the Brewers and jokingly told me that I should ask Brewers Manager Tom Trebelhorn about this obscure pitcher when he called to offer me a job. Not five minutes later my phone rang. The voice asked to speak with Doug Decatur and then told me it belonged to Tom Trebelhorn. I assumed the voice really belonged to one of the league members calling me to give me a hard time, so my initial reaction was, "Tom, great, I'm glad you called. I need to ask you about one of your pitchers." Eventually, though, it dawned on me that I was talking to the real Tom Trebelhorn and that I was about to become a statistical consultant for the Milwaukee Brewers.

Following in Part One are stories from my years as a statistical consultant with the Brewers, Reds and Cubs.

# Moe vs. Jose, Round 1 (1994 Cubs)

The Cubs' pitching coach was Moe Drabowsky. He was considered by many people, including Hank Bauer, his former manager, to be the star of the 1966 World Series thanks to his momentum-changing, record-setting, eleven-strikeout relief appearance in Game One of the Orioles' four-game sweep of the Dodgers. Drabowsky had come up with a chart for the Cubs' bullpen that used different colored stickers to signify the status of the pitchers: one color if a pitcher had just warmed up in a game, and others for outings of different lengths and/or pitch counts. The chart was somewhat useful, but to be honest it fell into the category of "too much information." Cubs Manager Tom Trebelhorn just wanted to know who was available in his bullpen each night, and the Cubs pitchers didn't need a chart to tell them whether or not they were tired.

At one point, we were in Atlanta to start a three-game series. Trebelhorn and I were going over my statistics scouting report on the Braves when Drabowsky came in wanting a place to set up his chart where his bullpen could see it. Trebelhorn wanted it some place they couldn't to avoid any grief from the pitchers. Drabowsky started to unfold and set up his chart right in the middle of the office, but Trebelhorn suggested Drabowsky set it up in an adjoining room—the manager's office bathroom. Drabowsky tried to resist, but Trebelhorn insisted that was the best place for it. So, disappointedly, Drabowsky set up shop in the bathroom.

A few minutes later, the Cubs' rubber arm reliever Jose Bautista came walking into Trebelhorn's office holding his arm, saying, "I no can pitch." "Why not?" Drabowsky demanded. Bautista replied, "I no can pitch." And then, referring to the now infamous chart and stickers, said, "I have two reds, a green, a blue and a yellow. I no can pitch." Drabowsky then tried to go through game by game with Bautista to figure out what colors he did have. Bautista would ward off every attempted explanation from Drabowsky with a shake of the head and a "I no can pitch." He proceeded to argue the color of each outing with Drabowsky and finally summed it all up by flatly stating, "Too many colors. I no can pitch." It became painfully obvious to Trebelhorn and me that Bautista was doing and saying whatever he could just to mess with Drabowsky, who took his colors and chart very seriously. Drabowsky stomped out to the bathroom to look at his chart. He came yelling back at Bautista that all he had in the last five days was one yellow. To that Bautista replied, "Oh, OK. One color. I pitch," and he walked out. At this point Drabowsky said, "That's exactly why we need the chart right in here where everyone can see it."

# Moe vs. Jose, Round 2 (1994 Cubs)

The day after his chart incident with Moe Drabowsky, Jose Bautista came into Tom Trebelhorn's office holding his arm and said, "I no can pitch." He then turned and showed us his arm. There was a big, red, baseball-sized circle on his arm complete with seam indents. Apparently Bautista had been shagging flies during batting practice and a ball bounced off the wall and ricocheted into him. Within seconds, Drabowsky had the Cubs' trainers and doctors working Bautista over like a prize fighter in his corner between rounds. All the while, Bautista was doing his best Meadowlark Lemon impersonation, "My arm, my arm. I no can pitch." I looked over at Trebelhorn and he just sat at his desk smiling and shaking his head. After a few minutes and a few more "I no can pitch" refrains from Bautista, Drabowsky's face turned bright red. "Jose," he screamed, "you're right handed!" Then he pointed to Bautista's left arm with the baseball imprint, "The ball hit your left arm." Bautista shrugged his shoulders and said, "Oh, OK, I pitch." He got up and walked out.

For the record, Jose Bautista was tied for second in the National League in games pitched (58) during the 1994 strike-shortened season. Many of Jose's appearances came that season on days during which Jose had informed Drabowsky minutes before a game that "I no can pitch."

# We're the Cubs! (1994 Cubs)

I was driving Tom Trebelhorn and several of the Cubs' coaches to a game in Atlanta. I found myself in the wrong lane, so I had to cut across a couple of lanes very quickly. Some guy, not liking my maneuver, honked and started screaming at me. Tom hung out the window waving his Cubs' hat and yelled, "It's OK. We're the Cubs." The guy stopped yelling and then waived and smiled. Tom explained it works every time because nobody hates the Cubs. Ever since that day my wife keeps a Cubs hat in her car just in case.

# A Cub Tree (1994 Cubs)

Now, I don't know for sure if this one is true or not, but the story goes that in 1994, when the Cubs' GM Larry Himes was interviewing managerial candidates, a psychology expert talked him into asking each candidate the following question: If you were a tree, what kind of a tree would you be? Apparently, the idea was that a qualified leader would answer that he was an oak tree—mighty and strong—or maybe an evergreen tree—a tree that stays strong and never loses its leaves. Himes figured what the heck? It couldn't hurt to ask the question. In the interviews, however, everyone was giving him the same oak tree or evergreen answers. The more tree answers he got, the more he thought that both the question and the answers were total crap. Eventually Himes interviewed Tom Trebelhorn and asked the tree question. Without hesitatation Trebelhorn responded, "A Chicago Cub tree." Himes hired him immediately.

# Greg Vaughn (1991-94 Brewers)

Everyone in baseball always has those "my boy" players—players who they recommend a team acquire, promote, and/or start. My first "my boy" player was Greg Vaughn. Vaughn was my first crusade with the Brewers. At the start of the 1991 season, the Brewers had elected to go with newly acquired Dante Bichette, Darryl Hamilton and Robin Yount in the outfield. Greg Vaughn was stuck on the Brewers' bench.

The first time I mentioned Vaughn to Brewers GM Harry Dalton, Dalton complained about Vaughn in every area. He said something about his arm being so bad that Vaughn was the only outfielder in the majors that required a relay man to warm up with the ball boy between innings. Later in his career Vaughn became one of the toughest left fielders to run on because of the fact that he charged base hits in front of him so well. Vaughn did a great job of working hard and turning a weakness into a strength.

At the time, however, I pushed hard for the Brewers to start Vaughn for two main reasons: One, Vaughn was projected by STATS Inc. to have a better season than Hamilton and Bichette:

**Hamilton:** .261 BA, 1 HR, .314 OBP, and .313 SLG for an OPS of .627
**Bichette:** .237 BA, 11 HR, .272 OBP, and .389 SLG for an OPS of .661
**Vaughn:** .243 BA, 20 HR, .310 OBP, and .440 SLG for an OPS of .751

Two, Vaughn was younger than both Hamilton and Bichette.

I sent the Brewers report after report, fax after fax, on why Vaughn should start from the first few weeks on. I argued every angle and submitted every fact I could find. After about three weeks, the Brewers finally gave in and Greg Vaughn became the Brewers' starting left fielder. There was an article in one of the Milwaukee papers I remember reading that stated that Vaughn was being moved into the Brewers' starting lineup. In the article, Manager Tom Trebelhorn stated that the reasons for making the switch from Hamilton to Vaughn had nothing to do with Hamilton's playing ability, but that he wanted to get Vaughn into the starting lineup. Trebelhorn listed a few reasons which were recited right out of one of my faxes. At the time, I had three thoughts: I fought hard to get Vaughn into the starting lineup and I had won; it was fun reading my arguments in the paper, even without credit; and I was making a difference. Of course, those thoughts quickly dissipated and were replaced with fears that Vaughn would completely fail and my career with the Brewers would be over quickly.

Vaughn, as it turned out, had a very good season, hitting 27 homers and driving in 98 runs. The next season, Vaughn started the year poorly and once again I sent fax after fax to new manager Phil Garner, urging him to resist the temptation to bench Vaughn. Garner kept telling me not to worry and that he was going to stick with Vaughn. The Brewers, however, were in a pennant race and it was hard not to bench a struggling hitter. I wanted to make sure that if there was any pressure from the top to send Vaughn back to the bench that Phil Garner would have the fire power to argue why he was sticking with Vaughn.

Now, I will never know if I had an impact on Greg Vaughn's career. We all like to think that the cream always rises to the top and that without my help Greg Vaughn would have eventually gotten the opportunity and had just as successful of a career. But you never know. Maybe if I hadn't pushed for a starting job for Vaughn he never would have gotten the opportunity to play every day. Maybe Vaughn's skills would have eroded sitting on the bench. Young players do have to play in order to develop. Again, we will never know whether or not I truly helped Greg Vaughn's career.

In 1993, just a few days before the All-Star break, Phil Garner and I were in the clubhouse when the American League President Bobby Brown walked in and said he needed to see one of the Brewers—Greg Vaughn. We walked through the clubhouse tunnel to the dugout and Garner called over Vaughn. Garner introduced him to Brown and trotted out onto the field. Brown said something to Vaughn, shook his hand, and headed back to the clubhouse. Vaughn just stood there, smiling like a man who had the greatest news in the world and was waiting for someone to tell. Realizing that Vaughn had just been told he had been named to the All-Star Team, I walked up to him with my hand outstretched and said congratulations. He had no idea who I was, but he shook my hand and practically gave me a hug. He was just thrilled there was someone there to share the moment.

I was almost as happy as Vaughn. Here was the first guy I ever put in a starting lineup, and now he was an All-Star. As I stood there all the faxes and reports I had sent to make Vaughn a starter and keep him there came to mind. I thought about telling Vaughn how I had helped his career, but standing there together in that moment, it seemed enough that I was the first to congratulate him on his selection.

# Tuffy (1994 Cubs)

In 1994, the Cubs had a center field leadoff hitter named Tuffy Rhodes. Rhodes hit three home runs on Opening Day that season. Even today, when an ordinary ballplayer has an extraordinary game, he is sometimes said to have had "a Tuffy Rhodes game." As wonderful as the occasional good game is for a player's morale, I contend that ordinary ballplayers don't do extremely good, cumulative things. An ordinary ballplayer may hit one big home run in a key game, but not in three key games. For example, Gene Tenace, who spent most of 1972 as a backup catcher, hit four home runs in the 1972 World Series, leaving everyone in Cincinnati who lost to Oakland that season asking how could an ordinary ballplayer do something like that. Well, it turned out that Tenace had a very good All-Star career and he wasn't very ordinary after all.

Furthermore, I told Cubs manager Tom Trebelhorn that Rhodes, like Tenace, was not going to have an ordinary career, but would go on to do bigger things. In early June of 1994, however, Rhodes was losing his confidence and getting down on himself. I pointed out this fact to Trebelhorn and suggested that Rhodes needed a vote of confidence. To my surprise, Trebelhorn called Rhodes into his office and told him that I wanted to talk to him. After I got over the initial shock, I told him how high the Cubs were on him and that he should just relax, go play, and have fun. He was our starting center fielder and we were sticking with him. When I was all done, Trebelhorn said, "OK, yes, you're my starting center fielder, but I'm starting Glenallen Hill today because a lefty is pitching. But, again, you are still the man." Well, Hill hit two home runs that day and instead he became the man.

A couple weeks after talking to Rhodes, my youngest son Joseph was born and I promptly nicknamed him Tuffy for two reasons: Tuffy Rhodes and I were both born in Cincinnati; and despite Glenallen Hill and my failed pep talk, I was convinced that Tuffy Rhodes was going to have an extraordinary career. Well, it did happen for Tuffy Rhodes, but just not in the United States. He went on to set the all-time single season home run mark in Japan.

# Trade Talks

**T**hree trade talk stories from the past:

(1) Once when Phil Garner was managing the Brewers, Garner and I were sitting in the dugout before a game in Cincinnati. Garner was telling me he wanted to unload Marquis Grissom's hefty salary. I pointed to the Reds GM Jim Bowden, who was standing on the field at the time, and said, "He'll take him. Bowden loves 'name players.'" So Garner hopped out of the dugout and went over to Bowden. They talked for just a few seconds and then Garner returned to the dugout, saying, "Reggie Sanders. Bowden said he would trade Sanders for Grissom right now. What do you know about Sanders?" "Well," I replied, "he is better than Grissom, but Sanders has had injury problems in the past." "Can't do it then," Garner answered. "We can't afford to pay guys who can't stay on the field." That was that.

(2) In 1994 the Brewers were planning a trade with the Baltimore Orioles. The Orioles wanted Jamie Navarro. The deal was basically worked out, but the Brewers wanted one more player. Brewers GM Sal Bando told me to give him a name of an Orioles minor league pitcher that could be added to the deal. Well, we didn't have any information with us at the time, no scouting reports, not even a copy of *Baseball America*. The only thing we did have was a listing of the Orioles' minor league statistics. I took a quick look at the numbers and gave Bando the name of the starting pitcher with the best walk/strikeout ratio—Jimmy Haynes. It turned out that Haynes was the Orioles' number one pitching prospect, and now they were insulted. Bando had to convince them that we weren't trying to pull a fast one and eventually got everything straightened out. When the Orioles GM called the Orioles owner for the OK, however, he was informed that the baseball strike was unavoidable and there was no sense trading a bunch of prospects to the Brewers in an effort to win this season when it would soon be over. That was the end of that deal.

*Note: Jimmy Haynes would post a 63-89 record in the majors. In 2004, Haynes was 0-3 with a 9.60 ERA with the Cincinnati Reds.*

(3) I don't know if this one is true or not, but there are people who were close to the Reds organization in the early sixties who tell me that the Reds had a GM who would "leak" potential trades to the press to see if the public would

approve of the deal or not. If the public liked the deal, it would go through. If the public didn't, the GM would pull the plug on that deal. Maybe he should have asked the public about that disastrous Frank Robinson for Milt Pappas deal.

# Junior's Batting Tip (1991-94 Brewers)

As manager of the Brewers, Phil Garner was constantly working with Greg Vaughn to hone his skills. In particular, Garner wanted to get Vaughn to wait on pitches a little longer. Vaughn kept pulling everything down the short left field line. Garner figured that Vaughn would throw away 10 to 20 home runs each year by pulling would-be home runs foul and he wanted Vaughn to drive the ball more to center or left-center. That way if Vaughn got a little out in front of a pitch, instead of hitting the ball foul the ball would stay fair for a home run. One day after playing a series with Seattle, Garner and I were sitting in his office when Vaughn walked in and said, "Look, I was talking with Junior [Ken Griffey] and Junior says he doesn't think about anything at the plate. He just swings. Maybe I should be doing the same."

Garner looked at Vaughn and said, "Vaughny, you know why that is?" He continued on, not waiting for an answer from Vaughn. "Junior's swing and his approach to hitting are perfect. If yours was perfect, you could just go up and swing also. But Vaughny, your swing is all bleeped up."

Vaughn just sighed, nodded, turned around, and walked out.

*Note: A few years later, during the 1998 season, Vaughn hit 50 home runs for the San Diego Padres.*

# Roberto Clemente (spring of 1967)

When I think of the Pirates, I can't help but think about the spring of 1967. I was in second grade and our family went to Fort Myers, Florida, for spring vacation. The Pirates held their spring training in Fort Myers and many of the players were staying at the same hotel where we were. One morning at breakfast I was complaining about how disappointed I was that I hadn't seen any Pirates at the hotel since we arrived. Of course, as a second grader, I was looking for players walking around in their uniforms. It never occurred to me that they would be in street clothes. Anyway, as I was in the middle of feeling sorry for myself, there was a tap on my shoulder. I looked around and there was Roberto Clemente sitting at the next table smiling at me. He wasn't wearing his uniform, but it was him. He asked me if I wanted his autograph. I said sure and my mother handed him a pen and paper. Around the table the paper went and my eyes grew bigger as I began to recognize both the faces and the names: Clemente, Willie Stargell, Maury Wills, Matty Alou, Jose Pagan, George Spriggs, and there were two others but I can no longer remember their names. What a thrill for an eight year old. Roberto Clemente didn't have to tap me on the shoulder and interrupt his breakfast to talk to me, but he did. Apparently, that's the kind of person Roberto Clemente was—the kind of person who five years later would tragically die helping others.

*Note: Clemente and Stargell are now in the Hall of Fame. Wills held the single season stolen base mark for a while until it was later broken by Lou Brock and then Rickey Henderson. Matty Alou won an NL batting title and is the brother of manager Felipe Alou.*

# Frank Robinson (winter of 1965-66)

When I was just a very young boy I would sort my baseball cards by teams—not by the team on the card, but by the team the players were currently with. The highlight of my week was when *The Sporting News* would arrive with that week's transactions. The night of the arrival of *The Sporting News*, my father would read the transactions aloud and I would write the player's new team on his card and put it with his new team. While for most kids my age, their favorite day of the year was Christmas, mine was June 15, the trading deadline. (It has since been pushed back to July 31.) The last week before the deadline there would be numerous trades, thus numerous changes to be made in my card arrangements. I loved trades. I remember I wanted more trades than would occur, so I would take my duplicate cards and make my own trades. Mostly I would trade second string Cincinnati Reds players, such as Chico Ruiz, for players like Willie Mays or Hank Aaron. My father would kid me that sooner or later, one of these trades I was making would come true and I would be sorry. Well, news came that the Reds had traded future Hall of Famer Frank Robinson for Milt Pappas. My father, disgusted by the trade, as were all Reds fans, joked that it must have been a trade I made with my cards that came true. Fighting back the tears I told him, "Dad, I would never make such a stupid trade." Understanding that he had hurt my feelings, and also knowing that even a little boy would not have made such a terrible trade, he replied, "I know, son. I know."

From that day on I wanted to be a general manager of a major league team. Other kids wanted to be doctors and policemen. I wanted to be a GM. I believed I had to be more qualified than the Reds GM Bill DeWitt who had traded Frank Robinson.

Frank Robinson is known for winning an MVP in both leagues, hitting 586 home runs, and for being the first African-American manager in major league history. Robinson is also responsible for one of the most quoted statements of all time: "Close [doesn't] count in baseball. Close only counts in horseshoes and grenades." Robinson's quote first appeared in *Time*, July 31, 1973.

## Sparky Anderson (summer of 1977)

In the summer of 1977, I worked in the little kiddy area at Kings Island, an amusement park just north of Cincinnati. One day Sparky Anderson, manager of the two-time World Champion Cincinnati Reds, showed up. I put the ride on auto pilot and went over to talk to Sparky. "Hi, Sparky. I know you guys are going to catch the Dodgers just like 1973," I began. It was August, the Reds were about ten games behind the Dodgers, but they had caught the Dodgers in 1973. Sparky smiled and said, "I got only three pitchers." That was true, and it was the reason the Reds were so far behind. I insisted that I had total confidence that somehow Sparky and the Reds were going to find a way to win. I told Sparky I wasn't giving up and that I was going to the game that very night.

Eventually I noticed that the kids on my ride were turning several shades of green, so I wished Sparky good luck that night and the rest of the season. Then it occurred to me that I was blowing my big chance to make a difference. Maybe I could give Sparky some advice that might turn the season around. My mind was racing. I couldn't come up with anything and out of desperation I blurted, "I really like Ed Armbrister, but he hardly ever plays." Immediately I thought to myself, 'What am I saying?' Ed Armbrister was a weak hitting, backup outfielder who couldn't field very well. Conversely, the 1977 Reds had a great starting outfield. They had George Foster in left, who was on his way to hitting 52 home runs that season and winning the NL MVP award. They had Ken Griffey, Sr., in right, who was an All-Star and was coming off a year where he finished second in the batting race. In center they had Cesar Geronimo who was in the middle of winning four straight Gold Gloves. Only a complete idiot would suggest that Armbrister should play more. But, in my moment of glory, that's what I did. Sparky smiled and, instead of calling me a complete idiot, responded with, "Bone chips." He then went on to explain that Ed Armbrister would be playing more if not for bone chips in his right elbow. Anyway, we said good-bye and I went back to stop my ride. I sat there thinking that maybe I wasn't so stupid. Maybe Sparky would play Armbrister more if not for the bone chips. Maybe.

When I got to the Reds' game that night, the Reds' starting right fielder was Ed Armbrister. As it turned out, that would be Armbrister's last start in the major leagues. Unfortunately, despite my brilliant advice to start Armbrister more, it didn't help the Reds any. They still finished ten games behind the Dodgers.

# My First Job in Baseball (1984 Reds)

In the fall of 1983, after finishing graduate school, I realized I really didn't want to be a financial analyst. I wanted to have a job in baseball. I wrote Reds GM Bob Howsam concerning a book by Bill James, *The Baseball Abstract*. I proposed that if the Reds would just apply some of Bill James' new theories on evaluating talent and building a winner, the Reds would gain a tremendous advantage over the rest of Major League Baseball.

Anyway, Howsam wrote me back and hooked me up with Greg Riddoch who was working in the Reds' front office at the time. Riddoch would go on to manage the San Diego Padres. He once told me that he was the Wally Pipp of Tampa (then the Reds' single A minor league team). Riddoch was Tampa's starting shortstop until they signed a kid named Dave Concepcion. Concepcion took over for Riddoch and went on to be the starting shortstop on the Big Red Machine in the 1970s. From there Riddoch went into coaching.

One of Riddoch's jobs was to supply Reds manager Vern Rapp with statistical information to help the Reds win ball games. The Reds had a bad ball club and Rapp was open to anything that would give the Reds an advantage. Thus I would send Riddoch information, theories and recommendations, and Riddoch, if he thought it was worthy of consideration, would send it on to Rapp. It was fun while it lasted. However, Bob Howsam had the opportunity to acquire Pete Rose and did so, naming Rose as a player/manager and Rapp was fired. Rose didn't have any use for statistics. Riddoch was reassigned and, consequently, my initial stint in baseball ended.

# Pete Rose (1985-89 Reds)

During the time Pete Rose was manager for the Reds, I wrote Rose, owner Marge Schott, and every GM Marge brought into Cincinnati. Despite the fact that Rose didn't care for statistics, sometimes the information I sent him would have an impact. For example, one early report I sent Rose indicated that the Reds would be better off if he only started himself against righthand pitchers. Rose responded by declaring himself in the newspaper "*not* a part-time player." Despite Rose's protest, however, from that day on he never started himself against a lefty pitcher for the rest of his career. I didn't learn until later about other effects I had on Rose. For example, after the Reds acquired Bill Gullickson, I sent Rose a letter questioning whether or not Gullickson could win with the Reds based on the fact that Gullickson's statistics in the prior few seasons on turf were poor and the Reds played their home games on turf. Later, when Rose was accused of betting on baseball, one of his accusers stated that Rose always bet on the Reds to win, but he would *not* bet at all when Gullickson pitched for the Reds.

Overall, Rose was a good manager and he did a good job of doing what was best for the team in the long run. He used to say, "I don't care what a player did in his last few at-bats, I want to know what he did in his last 500 at-bats." However, as far as bullpen use goes, Rose was clearly a short-run manager. When behind, conventional baseball wisdom dictates that a manager should just pitch his long man and mop-up man and let them finish out the game. The logic is that managers don't want to burn up their bullpen in a losing cause. Conversely, Rose would never give up on a game, especially in his last couple of seasons. Rose would manage every game like it was the postseason. Consequently, in his last two full seasons as Reds manager, he led the majors in pitching changes. In fact, Rose set an all-time record for pitching changes in 1987 with 392. This record has since been broken as teams have increased the number of pitchers on their rosters to first eleven and then twelve man staffs. However, my guess is Rose still holds the record for the most pitching changes in a season for a team using a 10-man staff.

On the average, a team wins about 15% of its games when trailing after six innings. The Reds won approximately 18% of those games during the 1987 and 1988 seasons. Thus, Rose's strategy netted the Reds about two extra come-from-behind wins a season. The problem with making so many pitching changes, however, is that the Reds' bullpen would get tired and become less effective. I remember a couple of the relievers voicing complaints. Lefty Rob Murphy was one of the guys who complained publicly. He was subsequently traded at the end of the 1988 season. In my opinion as a statistical consultant, I would have to say that the net effect of Rose's strategy for his bullpen use was that it cost the Reds a few more games than the two baseball games that it won. Whatever the case, it is clear Rose made all his pitching changes because he couldn't bear to give up on a game. What isn't clear is the reason he couldn't bear to give up on a game: Was it that he couldn't stand to lose, or was it that he couldn't stand to lose a bet?

# World Champs (1989-90 Reds)

During the 1989 season, I wrote Reds GM Murray Cook on several occasions, sending him statistical information and theories on the Reds. In late September of 1989, Cook asked to meet me in Atlanta at a Reds/Braves game. At the meeting, I gave Cook my game plan for turning the 1989 Reds into World Champions. The Reds needed a left fielder and a first baseman. Cook stated he was going to trade Reds pitcher Scott Scudder to the Cardinals for left fielder Vince Coleman. I told him he should trade Scudder to the Braves for infielder/outfielder Ron Gant and play Gant in left field and then sign first baseman Cecil Fielder (9 HR, .230 in 1988), who was spending the 1989 season playing in Japan. Cook argued that Gant couldn't hit enough to play the outfield. He was referring to the fact that Gant only hit .177 at the beginning of the season playing third base for the Braves before being demoted to AAA to learn how to play the outfield. There were four reasons, however, as to why I thought Gant was about to blossom as a hitter: one, Gant was now playing the outfield where he was comfortable and could just focus on hitting; two, Gant hit well in AAA after his demotion while playing the outfield; three, Gant had always hit in the minors and his offensive projections were good; and four, Gant had bulked up the previous winter. In 1988 while playing second base for the Braves, Gant had 36 doubles/triples. I expected that Gant's added muscle would turn the doubles and triples into home runs.

In the middle of our discussion on Gant, Gant hit a pitch deep into the seats in straight away center for a monster home run. Cook then turned to me, stuck out his hand, and said, "OK, we will do it. In a couple of weeks I will get my budget from Marge. I will see what I can pay you for next season and then we will go out and get Gant and Fielder." Two weeks later at the budget meeting Cook was fired.

The new Reds GM Bob Quinn fixed the Reds' two weaknesses by trading for Hal Morris to play first base and Billy Hatcher to play left field and the Reds won a World Championship. Fielder, by the way, did return to the United States and signed with Detroit. Gant won the starting left field job with the Braves. Here are the 1990 statistics for the players in question:

LF

| | | | |
|---|---|---|---|
| Coleman | 6 HR | .292 | Stayed with the Cardinals |
| **Gant** | **32 HR** | **.303** | **Stayed with the Braves** |
| Hatcher | 5 HR | .276 | Acquired by the Reds |

1B

| | | | |
|---|---|---|---|
| **Fielder** | **51 HR** | **.277** | **Signed by the Tigers** |
| Morris | 7 HR | .340 | Acquired by the Reds |

For the record, Gant and Fielder out-homered Hatcher and Morris 83 to 12, but Hatcher and Morris were enough to win the championship for the Reds. A few years later I was talking to Chuck Tanner, manager of the 1979 World Champion Pirates, who told me he had tried very hard to get the 1990 Reds' managerial position. He felt in 1989 the Reds were on the verge of a World Championship. Not to take anything away from the great job Reds GM Bob Quinn did winning a World Championship, but apparently there were a few of us who wanted a shot at the 1989/90 Reds.

# Rejection Letters (winter of 1990-91)

After my near miss with Murray Cook and the Reds and the subsequent World Championship for the Reds, I thought I might as well try other teams besides the Reds. Below are five of the rejection letters I received for my efforts.

## From the Philadelphia Phillies

Thank you for your letter inquiring about a statistical/analytical position with the Phillies. Though I found your facts interesting, at the present time I do not have any need for your services. Good luck with your endeavors. Thank you for your interest in the Phillies.

Sincerely,
Lee Thomas
Vice President/General Manager

*Note: Lee Thomas played with six teams in eight seasons in the majors and made the All-Star Team in 1962.*

## From the St. Louis Cardinals

Although we appreciate your interest in the Cardinals' organization, we feel our own personnel are on top of the situation. Although we do not feel a need to take advantage of your availability at the present time, we will be happy to hold your correspondence on file for consideration at a later date. Thank you for taking time to contact us. Best Wishes.

Sincerely,
Dal Maxvill
Vice President/General Manager.

*Note: Maxvill played in four World Series, including starting at shortstop for the World Champion Cardinals in 1964 and 1967.*

## From the Montreal Expos

At this time, the Expos are happy with the statistical information that we are receiving. However, your letter will be kept on file and should our situation change, your information will be reviewed. Thank you for your interest and best wishes to you and with your future baseball endeavors.

Sincerely,

Dave Dombrowski

Vice President, Player Personnel & General Manager

*Note: Dombrowski is currently the GM of the Detroit Tigers. In the 1990s the Expos were one of about only three or four teams that paid someone to provide them with statistical information and projections and also actually used the information. For a while in the 1990s the Expos were the model for a progressive, successful, talent-filled organization. I believe the 1994 baseball strike cost the Expos a trip to the World Series and led to the demise of the franchise.*

## From the California Angels

We have already begun the process of compiling data information through not only the club's resources but also via stats supplied from the office of the Commissioner of Baseball and, at this time, we do not foresee a need for those services mentioned. We appreciate your interest in the California Angels and hope that something good happens for you for the 1991 season. Kindest regards and best wishes.

Sincerely,

Daniel F. O'Brien

Senior Vice President Baseball Operations

*Note: O'Brien's son is currently the GM of the Reds. The Reds haven't been able to solve their pitching problems by "traditional methods," i.e., scouting and spending money. Despite the success that the small market Oakland Athletics have had by using advanced statistical information, the Reds have not followed suit.*

## From the Houston Astros

We have no interest in your services at this time.
    Sincerely,
    William J. Wood
    General Manager

# 40-19 (1991 Brewers)

One club didn't send me a rejection letter. The Milwaukee Brewers asked for a sample report. I completed one and sent it off as quickly as I could. Tom Trebelhorn, manager of the Milwaukee Brewers, responded with a phone call. Tom wanted me to work with him in Milwaukee. He hooked me up with Brewers GM Harry Dalton. Dalton's first words to me were, "We can't pay you this season. The budget is already done." Confident in my ability, I agreed to work for one season for free with the understanding that if they liked what I did for the Brewers, they would make it up to me the following season.

That year I sent the Brewers and Tom Trebelhorn over 200 reports and studies. Three years later, while managing the Cubs, Tom Trebelhorn told me he still had every single report and study I did. I submitted research reports on everything I could get my hands on: reports from STATS Inc., The Elias Baseball Analyst, Bill James, and others, plus my own studies and research. Many of the conclusions from the reports are in the GM IQ Test included in this book. The discussion in this book on bullpen use and batting order are two good examples of the type of information I sent the Brewers that season. I also sent statistical scouting reports on upcoming opponents. I pushed for lineup changes and roster moves. Greg Vaughn was inserted into the lineup and relief ace Doug Henry was pulled out of the minors thanks to my reports. The pitching staff was reshaped during the season and things began to start clicking with two months to go. The Brewers finished their last 59 games on a great run, going 40-19. This was almost identical to the 2004 Astros 40-18 finish. History shows that the team which finishes the season hot will see their winning ways carry over to the next season. Thus I felt confident the Brewers had a chance at a division title in 1992 and I was certain I had secured a job with the Brewers for the next season. 1992 was going to be a fun year.

However, a couple weeks after the season ended, Dalton and Trebelhorn were fired. After hearing the news of the firings, I remember sitting on my porch in a daze of disbelief. Nobody fires a manager when his team finishes the season on a 40-19 streak.

# Sal and Phil (1992-94 Brewers)

Sal Bando replaced the fired Harry Dalton as Brewers GM. I called Sal Bando to see what the Brewers would pay me for next season and Sal told me that he wasn't sure what I did, but he would keep me around for a year to see and that the Brewers would pay me whatever they paid me last season.

Phil Garner took over and as expected the Brewers continued where we left off the previous season. Again I busted my butt all season for the Brewers, sending Phil Garner approximately the same number and types of reports I sent Tom Trebelhorn the previous season. The Brewers finished second in their division with a 92-70 record.

The Brewers finally rewarded me for my hard work with a contract for 1993. At that time there were only three other statistical consultants working in Major League Baseball that I was aware of: Eddie Epstein in Baltimore, Craig Wright with Texas, and Mike Gimbel for the Montreal Expos. There was a general distrust of statistics in Major League Baseball. Most of the general managers were ex-ballplayers. The general belief among those GMs was that only those who had played the game were qualified for front office positions. This was a belief that "protected" those ex-jocks in front office positions. Now, however, according to a 2004 *Sports Illustrated* article, the belief in Major League Baseball is closer to 50/50—50% of the teams believe that the old school way of scouting and observation is the best way to evaluate baseball talent and the other 50% believe that statistics provide a more accurate way of evaluating players. Back in 1993, it was virtually 100% on the side of the old school.

# Working for the Cubs (1994 Cubs)

In 1994, the Cubs hired Tom Trebelhorn as manager and they quickly signed me on as a consultant for double what the Brewers were paying me, plus an on-line account with STATS Inc. The Brewers still had me under contract, so for the 1994 season I was working both for the Cubs and the Brewers. Mike Gimbel was also working for two clubs—the Expos and the Red Sox.

At midseason, I met with Cubs GM Larry Himes. Himes said he wanted me in Chicago full-time the next season working on player evaluation and contracts. My job would be to set up a system for the Cubs where every player was going to be evaluated based on their projected future value and their current market value. Our plan was to do a better job of evaluating players than the rest of baseball and get more out of our payroll than other clubs. We had visions of taking the Cubs to the World Series.

However, after the 1994 season, a change in power at the Chicago Tribune resulted in a change of control of the Cubs. Larry Himes and Tom Trebelhorn were both fired. History speaks well of Larry Himes, who forever is known in Chicago as the man who twice traded for Sammy Sosa and insisted that Sosa play every day. Unfortunately for Himes, the Cubs and myself, Himes was not around with the Cubs to enjoy the bat of Sosa when he finally developed as a hitter.

After this latest string of disappointments, I came to the conclusion that baseball just wasn't ready for the advanced use of statistics. The old guard was entrenched in its power and it appeared that they would stay in power for the near future. Thus, by the time the baseball strike ended in the spring of 1995, I had already decided to end my run for a job in Major League Baseball.

# John Smiley's Shoes (summer of 1996)

I was sitting beside the pool at our apartment complex watching my oldest son swim. One of his playmates in the pool was Madison Burba, daughter of Reds pitcher Dave Burba. Dave's wife, Star Burba, was talking with some Reds fans who were jokingly giving her a hard time about her husband's win/loss record. Star defended her husband, stating that he had been pitching well, but he wasn't getting any run support.

I told Star that I had a formula that neutralizes the effects of run support and would calculate the win/loss record a pitcher would be expected to have based on average run support. This was a formula I came up with while working on Jamie Navarro's arbitration case for the Brewers. The formula is based in part on Bill James' Pythagorean winning percentage formula. Star told me Dave would be interested in such a formula. I offered to crunch the numbers for Dave and drop off the calculations at their apartment along with the formula and explanation. I did just that.

A day later, I was shooting baskets on the complex's basketball court and Dave came over. He said he loved the formula and he wanted to hook me up with his agent Myles Shoda. I ended up working that year for Shoda on Dave Burba and also on John Smoltz, who was another client of Shoda's. John Smoltz ended up signing the biggest contract ever for a pitcher at that time.

Dave Burba stories:

(1) One of the things I found interesting in my conversations with Dave was that he questioned me on how management evaluated pitchers. Dave wanted to know exactly what management wanted so he could try to increase his value. We also talked about his conversion from a relief pitcher to a starter. I told Dave the increase in innings pitched could cause arm problems. He told me that Myles Shoda had him undergo a test to identify his weakest muscles, muscles that were most likely to be susceptible to injury. Then he was put on an exercise program to strengthen the identified weaker muscles.

(2) Dave gave us tickets one night that he was pitching. When Dave came up to bat, I pointed out to my four year old that Madison's daddy was batting. My son looked at Burba, looked at me, and said, "Daddy, when do you get to bat?"

(3) At the end of the season, Dave said he had about ten pairs of John Smiley's size-13 Cincinnati Reds shoes that Smiley had given Burba when Smiley was traded from the Reds. The shoes were a little too big for Burba, but since they were my size, he wanted me to have them. Apparently, Smiley had a pretty good shoe connection. Anyway, we went back to Dave's apartment and his wife had already moved everything for the offseason. Dave's apartment was empty except for one thing, a baseball bat. Dave laughed and said she knows better than to move my "home run" bat. Dave had hit a home run that season. So much for the John Smiley shoes.

*Note: After the 2004 season, Dave Burba signed a minor league contract with the Astros. Now maybe I can finally get that pair of shoes.*

# Game Reports (1991-94 Brewers)

The old days with the Brewers revisited: Before each Brewers series I would send Phil Garner a statistical scouting report on the opposing team. Sections included:

- The ideal type of batter for each of our opponents' pitchers.
- The ideal type of pitcher for each of our opponents' hitters, including which of our relievers were best suited to get each hitter out.
- Percentage of base stealers thrown out by our opposing catcher.
- The base stealing percentage against each of the opposing pitchers, including balks and pickoffs.
- The stolen base percentage of each opposing hitter.
- The sacrifice hits, sacrifice attempts, sacrifice percentage, and the bunt for hits totals for each opposing hitter.
- A chart listing opposing pitchers based on those best suited to hit and run against based on several key factors (walks, strikeouts, home runs, and groundouts allowed) that affected hit-and-run success rates.
- Which opposing baserunners were most affected by throws to first.
- Managerial tendencies.
- Anything else I thought might help win a game.

I didn't really like doing these reports because I wanted to spend my time working to help GM Sal Bando acquire players who would improve the Brewers. I finally decided that I would just quit sending them, figuring that probably no one was reading them anyway. That resulted in a phone call from Phil from the dugout at Yankee Stadium during the national anthem wanting to know where the report was. So I started doing them again. My understanding now is that almost all major league teams receive some type of statistical pregame or preseries reports.

# Radar Gun (1991-94 Brewers)

Today in Major League Baseball the scoreboard lists the speed of every pitch. In the 1990s, the speed of pitches had to be signaled into the dugouts. Managers would always want to know when a pitcher began to lose his velocity. Apparently, Phil Garner still checks the numbers, because during the 2004 playoffs Brandon Backe kept looking to check his speed on the scoreboard. Backe wanted to make sure that he wasn't losing any speed and giving Phil an excuse to yank him from the game.

Back in the early 1990s, I had radar gun duty during a game for the Brewers. A couple of the players, pitcher Ricky Bones and infielder Pat Listach, kept asking me to signal in the speed of every pitch. Now I was only supposed to signal in the speed when a pitching change was made or it was getting late in the game. Bones and Listach were bored, however, and were making friendly wagers on the speed of each pitch. I didn't want to keep Ricky and Pat from having a little fun so I signaled in each pitch all game long. Then in the eighth inning, just about the time Phil needed a pitcher's speed, I found out why we didn't signal in each pitch all game—the battery on the gun went dead. This caused a lot of laughing and snickering out of Listach and Bones and a lot of grumbling from Phil.

A few more words on Pat Listach. He was a basically a one-year-wonder for the Brewers, stepping in at shortstop in 1992 and winning the AL Rookie of the Year Award. Listach was one of the nicest players on the Brewers. Every time I was with the club he made it a point to stop by and say hello. In fact, Pat was such a nice guy I kind of hated sending all those reports to GM Sal Bando that concluded with "Get rid of Listach. He stinks." Listach finished his career with the Houston Astros in 1997.

# Paul Molitor (1992-93 Brewers)

Paul Molitor left the Brewers after the 1992 season to become a free agent. Molitor signed with the Blue Jays, who went on to win the World Series that season. Conversely, the Brewers haven't had a winning season since Molitor left. Here is the story behind Molitor leaving.

After the 1992 season, both Robin Yount and Paul Molitor were free agents. Brewers owner Bud Selig told GM Sal Bando that he was only authorized to sign one of the two players. I was told that Bud wanted to use the loss of either Yount or Molitor to drive home his point that small market teams could not compete against the large market clubs. In defense of Bud, the absence of meaningful revenue sharing in baseball is absurd, but that is another discussion for another time. Both Yount and Molitor were willing to sign with the Brewers for much less than they were expected to get on the open market. Selig stuck to his guns, however. He wanted to make a point. Sal took a poll of all the key people in the organization asking them who they thought the Brewers should keep—Molitor or Yount. I said Molitor.

Sal told me that I was only one to say Molitor. Apparently everyone else came to the conclusion that the Brewers just couldn't let a man like Yount, who had 3,000 hits, walk. I said that I would much rather have the player who was still going to get 3,000 hits than the one who had most of his hits behind him. Bando felt that the fans wouldn't forgive the Brewers if they let go of Yount. I told him they would have a harder time forgiving a losing team than they would the loss of Yount. Needless to say, I was overruled.

At the eleventh hour, Bud Selig decided that he just couldn't bare to lose Molitor either, and he made a desperate attempt to sign him. Paul Molitor had too much pride to sign with the Brewers at that point. The Brewers had previously told him no, and he just couldn't get over that fact.

# Chuck Tanner (1992 Brewers)

Chuck Tanner was the manager of the 1979 World Champion Pittsburgh Pirates, a team that included a second baseman named Phil Garner. When Phil was hired to manage the Brewers, Chuck was hired as a consultant to Phil in 1992. I got to meet Chuck Tanner that season and I can honestly say that I probably had more fun talking with Chuck Tanner than anyone I ever met in baseball. Chuck spent one day telling me old baseball stories. It was great hearing about the good old days. I remember asking him what made him decide to start little-used pitcher Jim Rooker in Game Five of the World Series with the Pirates down 3-1, and Chuck told me simply that he knew Rooker wouldn't be bothered by the situation. He would just go out and pitch. Rooker did and the Pirates came back and won the 1979 Series.

Have you ever had one of those discussions where you and your friends are sitting around arguing who was the starting left fielder for some team in some year? I once got into one of those discussions with Chuck Tanner, Phil Garner and Tim Foli. We started arguing over who was the 1979 Pirates' left fielder. I said it was Bill Robinson, but Chuck, Phil and Tim said it was Mike Easler. At one point Phil or Tim pointed out that I was arguing with the manager (Chuck), the second baseman (Phil), and the shortstop (Tim) of the team in question. I should just concede and admit they were right. I refused. We then went looking for Easler, who at the time was the Brewers' hitting coach, but failed to find him. Instead, we looked up Easler's batting record in a media guide. Easler, it turned out, batted only 54 times that season. I was right and Robinson was actually the Pirates' starting left fielder that season. Never argue statistics, I pointed out to Chuck, Phil, and Tim, with a statistical consultant.

# On the Docks

When Harry Dalton was fired as Milwaukee Brewers GM, the thought was that Assistant General Manager Bruce Manno would be named GM. Bruce had been responsible for building up the Brewers' minor league system that won Baseball America's award for the top minor league system three years in a row (1985, 1986, 1987).

However, Bruce was passed over and the Brewers named former Oakland A's third baseman Sal Bando as GM. This was not an unusual decision for the early nineties in baseball. Most of the GMs were either ex-ballplayers or relatives of previous GMs. Bruce Manno was neither and, as I mentioned before, the thought throughout baseball at the time was that only the people who had played the game at the major league level could truly evaluate talent. This was unfortunate for the Brewers, because Bruce would have been a fine GM, and it was probably unfortunate for me because at some point I might have become his assistant GM. As it was, Bruce remained Sal's assistant GM until the baseball strike hit. The strike forced the Brewers to make cutbacks and Bruce was let go.

I remember meeting Bruce at a Denny's in Milwaukee for lunch one summer. Neither one of us had a job that was worth a damn. Bruce was working at a loading dock in Milwaukee. I'm not sure which lousy job I was working at the time. We both agreed it was hard to be motivated to forge ahead on any type of real career outside of baseball when your heart belongs to the game.

Bruce told me about a project he was working on that he believed would get him back in baseball. I even helped him prepare for an interview by researching the team in question and helping him prepare his game plan.

Well, Bruce caught a break and was hired as the Assistant General Manager in Baltimore. Then he received a bad break when changes in the power structure in Baltimore caused him to be pushed aside, forcing him to move on to the St. Louis Cardinals as their Director of Player Development. I haven't talked to Bruce in a couple of years, but I am happy that he has found a new home in baseball where he belongs.

# A Rockie Interview (winter of 1999-2000)

After Phil Garner was fired from Milwaukee he interviewed with several teams. One of the teams was the Rockies. Phil and I talked before his interview and Phil asked me for a game plan to get the Rockies into contention that he could discuss at the interview. I told Phil that most people would say work on improving the Rockies' pitching staff. However, Colorado is such a good hitters park and such a bad pitchers park that it skews everyone's statistics. More specifically, the Rockies' hitters are not nearly as good as their raw statistics would indicate. My strategy would be to trade a couple of the Rockies over-priced, over-valued hitters for younger, less expensive hitters who would hit even better than the Rockies' current high priced hitters.

Well, the Rockies didn't hire Phil. But soon after Phil's interview the Rockies traded two of their high priced veteran hitters, Vinny Castilla and Dante Bichette, and replaced them with cheaper, younger, better hitters. Maybe Phil and I should have asked the Rockies for a consulting fee.

# Maksudian's Ass (1994 Cubs)

In the top of the fourth inning of Game Five of the Astros/Braves 2004 Division Series, Jeff Kent dove headfirst into first base on a groundout to short. Announcer Steve Lyons commented that sliding headfirst into first base has been proven to take longer than merely running through the bag.

A couple of points worth noting here: (1) Phil Garner told me that when Kent was younger, management (of whichever team he was with at the time) complained to Kent that he wasn't hustling. Kent has a sort of laid back style that was being misinterpreted as a lack of hustle. To combat this misconception by management, Kent began diving headfirst into first on close plays. This made management happy and kept them off Kent's back, so unfortunately it became a habit for him that he now can't seem to break. (2) The play-by-play announcer who was working the game with Lyons, I think it was Joe Buck, commented something to the effect that at least Kent dusted himself off the right way. Buck's comment was a reference to Lyons, who once dove into first and then in an effort to clean himself off dropped his pants in the middle of the game. Lyons refused to bite on Buck's comment. I guess Lyons would like to forget about the pants dropping incident, although it is one everyone else can't seem to forget.

Here is another pants dropping incident concerning Lyons that is a little less famous. In 1994, Lyons was doing an interview in the Cubs' dugout before the game with Mike Maksudian, a third-string catcher for the Cubs. I happened to be in the dugout at the same time. Lyons asked Maksudian if it was true that he had a tattoo of every major league team's logo for which he had played—Twins, Blue Jays and Cubs. Maksudian said it was true. Lyons asked to see them. Maksudian replied, "Well, they're on my ass." Lyons insisted he needed proof, then asked me if I wanted to see them also. I declined—there was a limit to what I was willing to do to advance myself in baseball. Kissing management's ass is one thing. Looking at Maksudian's ass is another.

Years later I asked my wife why I fell short of my dream to one day be a general manager of a major league team. She replied that I didn't go that extra yard…I should have looked at Maksudian's ass.

# PART TWO

# THE GM IQ TEST

> # Part A – Multiple Choice (1-40)
>
> # Part B – True or False (41-80)
>
> # Part C – Formulas (81-90)
>
> # Part D – Real-Life Applications (91-100)

*"Aww, I don't want to hear any statistics. I see what's going on with my own eyes."*
— Joe Schultz, Manager of the 1969 Seattle Pilots

Up until recently, most managers and GMs in baseball were like Joe Schultz—they didn't put a lot of credence in statistics. Major League Baseball, however, has changed. In the recent bestseller *Moneyball*, author Michael Lewis describes how Oakland Athletics GM Billy Beane uses statistical information to put together winning teams every year despite a small payroll. In July of 2004, the Houston Astros hired Phil Garner as their manager and Garner used advanced statistical theories to enable the Astros to jump over five teams and steal the National League Wild Card (the 2004 Astros will be discussed in detail in Part Three of this book).

The point is, in today's baseball environment both GMs and managers must have a good working knowledge of baseball statistics in order to be successful. Consider this 1984 quote from Bill James:

*"[O]ther things being equal, a manager with respect for knowledge is going to beat the crap out of a manager who doesn't. And that's why sabermetrics [the study of baseball statistics] is an inevitable part of baseball's future."*

Bill James was hired by the Boston Red Sox as their Senior Baseball Operations Advisor prior to the 2004 season, a season in which the Red Sox won their first World Championship since 1918.

Now, do you think you can match wits with the likes of Manager Phil Garner, GM Billy Beane and Advisor Bill James? Phil Garner scored a 97% on the quiz. Can you do better? Well, here is your chance. I must warn you, however, that this test is not easy. If the only sports publication you read has a swimsuit edition, you're probably not going to do very well. As far as statistical knowledge goes, this test will separate the men from, well, you get the idea.

Pencils ready?

Good luck.

## Question 1

The correlation between total team runs and which spot in the batting order is the strongest:

(A) leadoff
(B) second
(C) cleanup
(D) 8th in NL and 9th in AL

# Answer 1

**(B)** second

From the *1986 Baseball Abstract:* "[T]he correlation of runs scored in the number two slot to the total runs scored by the team is closer than for any other position—that is, the teams which got a lot of runs out of their number two hitters, also got a lot of runs period."

There are two explanations here from the *Abstract:* (1) "This could also be taken to reflect the marginal nature of the position. Everybody has at least one good hitter to hit third, so that doesn't tell you that much about the offense, but the only teams which have good hitters hitting second are those which have five good hitters, hence score lots of runs." (2) "[M]any managers tend to waste the second spot in the order by putting somebody there who isn't one of the better hitters on the team....Too many managers will say 'bat control' as if these words were a magic wand, and place some .260 hitter with a secondary average of .150 batting second...."

## Question 2

What would happen if a team of Gold Glove winners played a team of Silver Sluggers:

(A) the Gold Glove team would win
(B) the Silver Slugger team would win
(C) Gary Sheffield would refuse to play in the game without first receiving compensation

# Answer 2

**(B)** the Silver Slugger team would win

From John Dewan's Stat of the Week™, November 10, 2004: "The difference between an average hitter and the best hitters is larger than the difference between an average fielder and the best fielders." Thus, all other things equal, the Silver Sluggers would be a more successful team than the Gold Glovers. Dewan ran computer simulations (using Strat-O-Matic's computer baseball game) of a league comprised of Silver Slugger teams and Gold Glove teams. The results were as expected—the Silver Slugger teams far out performed the Gold Glove teams.

## Question 3

Which team would be expected to win the most games:

(A) a team which scores 1000 runs and allows 900 runs
(B) a team which scores 800 runs and allows 700 runs
(C) a team which scores 600 runs and allows 500 runs
(D) all teams will win the same number of games

# Answer 3

**(C)** a team which scores 600 runs and allows 500 runs

For this one use the Pythagorean Formula for baseball developed by Bill James:

$$\text{Wins} = (\text{Runs Scored}^2) / (\text{Runs Scored}^2 + \text{Runs Allowed}^2) * 162$$

A team scoring 600 runs and allowing 500 runs would win 96 games. A team scoring 800 runs and allowing 700 runs would win 92 games and a team scoring 1000 runs and allowing 900 runs would win 90 games.

## Question 4

How many runs do the best and worst baserunners individually add or subtract over the course of a season?

(A) less than 5
(B) 5 to 10
(C) 11 to 15
(D) 16 to 20

## Answer 4

**(B)** 5 to 10

From *Baseball Prospectus 2005*: "In the most extreme cases, baserunning can add up to close to 10 runs per season, or about one win, not an insignificant amount when evaluating players. More frequently, however, the best and worst baserunners only add and subtract about five runs over the course of a season."

# Question 5

The stolen base success rate breakeven point is approximately:

(A) 50%
(B) 60%
(C) 70%
(D) 80%

# Answer 5

**(C)** 70%

There have been several studies on this one. The last one I saw put the breakeven point at approximately 70%. There is an inverse relationship between home runs and stolen bases. When home runs and runs are easy to come by, stolen bases go down. There is no reason to risk a steal when there is a good chance that the next hitter will hit a home run. Thus, when the home run rate is very high, the stolen base breakeven point has to go up a bit.

*Note: The stolen base success rate for Major League Baseball in 2005 was 71%.*

## Question 6

Because players tend to gravitate towards this position as they age, in most cases this is a position NL teams should probably NOT tie up with a long-term contract:

(A) shortstop
(B) center field
(C) first base
(D) bullpen coach

# Answer 6

**(C)** first base

First base is the last stop for aging good hitters in the National League. Players peak earlier defensively than they do offensively, which means good NL hitters, as they age, are destined for first base. For example, since Sean Casey became the Reds' first baseman, the Reds have had to trade Paul Konerko when Konerko had to be moved from third to first and Dmitri Young when Young had to be moved from outfield to first. Presently the Reds have Adam Dunn, who looks more like a first baseman every year, and Ken Griffey, Jr., who has chronic leg problems and might be better off at first. Going back 30 years, the Reds have had to make four tough decisions in one ten-year period at first base. In 1972, the Reds moved Tony Perez from third to first and traded Lee May. In 1977, the Reds moved Dan Driessen from third to first and traded Tony Perez. In 1979, Pete Rose needed to be moved from third to first and the Reds kept Driessen and let Rose go. And in 1981, Johnny Bench could no longer catch and wanted to be moved to first, but again the Reds went with Driessen, forcing Bench into a failed attempt to play third and, consequently, ultimately forcing him into retirement. Dan Driessen can tell his grandchildren that the Reds selected him over two Hall-of-Famers: Tony Perez and Johnny Bench, and also that Pete Rose guy.

Regardless, the significance of this question is two-fold: (1) players will be moving to first as they age; and (2) a GM needs to be extra careful concerning long-term deals at first base.

## Question 7

Statistically, hitters are the most effective when:

(A) a stolen base is attempted during their at-bat
(B) a stolen base is not attempted during their at-bat
(C) George Steinbrenner sends them a memo telling them they stink

## Answer 7

**(B)** a stolen base is not attempted during their at-bat

From the *1993 Baseball Scoreboard*: "[H]itters are most effective when a stolen base is *not* attempted." The numbers for the 1992 season: In stolen base situations, batters hit .271 when a stolen base was not attempted and .235 when a stolen base was. "[T]he hitter has often fallen behind on the count, or even swung and missed deliberately, in order to give the runner a chance to steal."

## Question 8

The best predictor of future success by a pitcher is his prior season's:

(A) ERA
(B) winning percentage
(C) baserunners per inning
(D) strikeouts to walks ratio

# Answer 8

**(D)** strikeouts to walks ratio

This fact is in just about every book Bill James ever wrote. In the *1995 Bill James Player Rating Book*, James listed this as one of his top ten "key things I know." "Make a list of pitchers with good strikeout/walk ratios but poor overall records….You'll find that their overall records, as a group, will be better next year than it was this year. Do the opposite—pitchers with good records but bad strikeout ratios and check them next year. You'll see that, as a group, they've collapsed."

## Question 9

The average batting average in Major League Baseball is the lowest when:

(A) there are no outs
(B) there is one out
(C) there are two outs
(D) there is drug testing

## Answer 9

**(C)** there are two outs

From John Dewan's Stat of the Week™, June 9, 2005: "Here are the batting averages in the majors over the last three and half years: 0 outs .273; 1 out .268; and 2 outs .250."

## Question 10

In general, the more times a pitcher throws to first:

(A) the lower a baserunner's stealing percentage
(B) the higher a baserunner's stealing percentage
(C) a baserunner's stealing percentage stays relatively the same, however beer sales increase as fans become bored with each additional throw to first

# Answer 10

**(A)** the lower a baserunner's stealing percentage

From the *1992 Baseball Scoreboard:* "If throwing to first were essentially meaningless, one would expect to find little difference—or random year-to-year variations—between the two situations....The numbers, though, have been remarkably consistent. In each of the three seasons we've studied the issue, throwing to first has helped cut down on the stolen base success rate."

When I was with the Brewers in the early 1990s we told our pitchers to throw to first more often as a result of this information, especially against the baserunners who were affected the most statistically by the throws to first. However, I never did check on whether or not beer sales went up as we increased our throws to first.

# Question 11

All groups of players (except knuckleball pitchers) reach their peak value at what age:

(A) 27
(B) 29
(C) 30
(D) 32

## Answer 11

**(A)** 27

From *This Time Let's Not Eat the Bones:* "[A]ll groups of players (except knuckleball pitchers and those specifically selected because they had their best years at some other age) reach their peak value at the age of twenty-seven and decline thereafter. The peak period for ballplayers is not twenty-eight to thirty-two, as was once believed, but twenty-five to twenty-nine. Almost every accomplishment (twenty-win seasons, hundred-RBI seasons, winning a batting championship, winning a Gold Glove, etc.) is more common at age twenty-seven than any other age."

## Question 12

A pitcher who allows a lot of flyballs but not many home runs will in the next season:

(A) see his performance regress
(B) see his performance improve
(C) see little or no change in performance
(D) sign with the Cincinnati Reds to help teach Eric Milton how not to give up a home run

## Answer 12

**(A)** see his performance regress

From *Baseball Prospectus 2005*, "A pitcher that allowed a lot of flyballs but not many home runs would be a pretty good bet to see his performance regress in the next season, for example, as some of those warning track shots went over the fence."

## Question 13

Good teams outscore poor teams by the greatest margin in which three innings:

(A) the first three innings
(B) the middle three innings
(C) the last three innings
(D) approximately the same margin in each of the three inning intervals

## Answer 13

**(D)** approximately the same margin in each of the three inning intervals.

From *This Time Let's Not Eat the Bones:* "Good teams outscore poor teams or average teams in the first three innings and the middle three innings by just as much as in the late three innings…." A study examining this issue was published in the *1983 Baseball Abstract*. A related study was published by Scott Segrin in the June 1985 edition of *Baseball Analyst*.

## Question 14

Players who hit for a higher than career batting average in a given season will most likely:

    (A) continue to improve their batting average the following season
    (B) see their batting average decline the following season
    (C) repeat their performance the following season
    (D) hold out for a new contract

## Answer 14

**(B)** see their batting average decline the following season

From *This Time Let's Not Eat the Bones:* "Players who hit for a high batting average in any season have a powerful tendency to decline in batting average in the next season. [This is] among the many consequences of the Law of Competitive Balance, which is discussed at length in the *1983 Baseball Abstract* pages 220-222."

## Question 15

Historically, converting an outfielder into a third baseman is successful approximately:

(A) 100% of the time
(B) 75% of the time
(C) 50% of the time
(D) 25% of the time

## Answer 15

**(D)** 25% of the time

From *This Time Let's Not Eat the Bones:* "Steven Goldleaf studied the issue and concluded that the outfield-to-third base conversion was successful about one-fourth of the time.... However, Steven was awfully generous in determining what was a successful conversion, and used a standard for inclusion in the study which automatically eliminated many of the most dramatic failures. It would seem to me that an estimate of 5 percent success would be as reasonable as 25 percent."

## Question 16

Over time what percentage of players hit better with a platoon advantage:

    (A) 65-70%
    (B) 75-80%
    (C) 85-90%
    (D) 95-100%

## Answer 16

**(D)** 95-100%

From the *1988 Baseball Abstract:* "The data as a whole leaves little doubt but that almost every player, if studied over a long enough period of time, would hit better with than without the platoon advantage."

## Question 17

The following is true about power pitchers versus finesse pitchers:

(A) power pitchers pitch better in September than finesse pitchers
(B) finesse pitchers pitch better in April than power pitchers
(C) both A and B are true
(D) neither A nor B is true

## Answer 17

**(C)** both A and B are true

From a study in the *1986 Baseball Abstract:* "[H]ard throwers throughout the study struggled in April" and "Power pitchers were markedly more effective in…September." Winning percentages for pitchers in the study overall were .610 for both. Finesse pitchers were .630 in April and .580 in September. Power pitchers were .490 in April and .654 in September.

## Question 18

What is the percentage of non-pitchers winning the Rookie of the Year Award who have gone on to have Hall of Fame careers:

(A) 10%
(B) 20%
(C) 33%
(D) 50%

## Answer 18

**(C)** 33%

From *This Time Let's Not Eat the Bones:* "[A]bout one-third of players who win the Rookie of the Year Award will have brilliant careers and eventually go into the Hall of Fame." This study can also be found in the *1987 Baseball Abstract.*

## Question 19

On average, what percentage of a team's assists is recorded by shortstops:

(A) 18%
(B) 28%
(C) 38%
(D) 48%

## Answer 19

**(B)** 28%

From the *Historical Baseball Abstract:* "A shortstop in modern baseball normally records about 28% of his team's assists—actually 28.3%."

## Question 20

The number of runs a team scores is essentially a function of a team's:

(A) stolen bases and home runs
(B) on-base percentage and slugging percentage
(C) hits and opponents' errors
(D) at-bats minus strikeouts

## Answer 20

**(B)** on-base percentage and slugging percentage

From the *1995 Bill James Player Ratings Book:* "The number of runs a team scores is essentially a function of two things: the number of men on base, and the team slugging percentage." This fact is the basis for Bill James' Runs Created per Game Formula. To do a quick and dirty check for a given team for a season, take a team's ABs times their on-base percentage times their slugging percentage and you will come somewhat close to their runs scored.

## Question 21

In sac-fly situations as opposed to all situations, major league hitters as a group:

- (A) hit a higher percentage of flyballs
- (B) hit the same percentage of flyballs
- (C) hit a lower percentage of flyballs

# Answer 21

**(B)** hit the same percentage of flyballs

From the *1993 Baseball Scoreboard:* "[P]layers don't hit a medium-to-long fly when they're trying to do so any more often than when they're not." The numbers: 17.6% in sac fly situations versus 17.7% in all other situations.

## Question 22

Statistically, the best sacrifice bunt situation is:

(A) man on first
(B) man on second
(C) men on first and second
(D) men on first and third

## Answer 22

**(C)** men on first and second

From the *1993 Baseball Scoreboard:* "With a runner on first only, the sacrifice is a losing proposition unless one run (and no more) is badly needed. However, data from 1987 through 1989 indicates that sacrificing with men on first and second is a good percentage move unless a very good hitter is at the plate."

## Question 23

Based on data from the 1965-88 drafts, which region has the *best* rate of return in terms of value per pick:

(A) California
(B) Florida
(C) Great Lakes Region

## Answer 23

**(C)** Great Lakes Region

See the answer to Question 24.

## Question 24

Based on data from the 1965-88 drafts, which region has the *worst* rate of return in terms of value per pick:

(A) California
(B) Florida
(C) Great Lakes Region

## Answer 24

**(B)** Florida.

Rate of returns from *The Baseball Abstract Newsletter,* Special Issue #1: The Northern Industrial States and Great Lakes Region (1.21); California (1.16); New England (1.00); Pacific Northwest (.64); and the South (.61). Included in the South is Florida with a return of (.42).

## Question 25

Research has shown that a typical player hits doubles or triples in 6% or 7% of his balls in play (at-bats minus home runs and minus strikeouts). There are two distinct types of players who fall below 6%. They are:

(A) superstars and marginal players
(B) slap hitters and slow runners
(C) home run hitters and fast runners
(D) Cubs and Red Sox

# Answer 25

**(B)** slap hitters and slow runners

From the *Bill James Historical Baseball Abstract:* "There are two distinct types of players who fall below 6%: slap hitters, and slow runners. There is little overlap between these two groups, and there are few players for whom it is difficult to say whether this guy has a low percentage because he is a slap hitter, or because he is slow. Why? Because there is nobody who is both a slap hitter and a slow runner.... [Y]ou cannot be both slow and a slap hitter, and play in the major leagues for any length of time."

# Question 26

Based on the drafts from 1965-88, what is true concerning draft picks invested in college players versus draft picks invested in high school players:

- (A) draft picks invested in college players yielded a rate of return essentially twice that of draft picks invested in high school players
- (B) draft picks invested in high school players yielded a rate of return essentially twice that of draft picks invested in college players
- (C) draft picks invested in high school and in college players yielded approximately the same return
- (D) none of the above

## Answer 26

**(A)** draft picks invested in college players yielded a rate of return essentially twice that of draft picks invested in high school players.

From *This Time Let's Not Eat the Bones:* "In the years 1965-88, draft picks invested in college players yielded a rate of return essentially twice that of draft picks invested in high school players."

## Question 27

What is the average "Save" conversion rate for "Tough Saves," "Regular Saves," and "Easy Saves"? The definitions: a Tough Save situation occurs when a pitcher enters the game with the tying run on base. An Easy Save situation occurs when a pitcher enters the game with at least a two run lead, no one on base, and pitches one inning or less. All other saves are Regular Saves.

(A) 20% - 50% - 90% (Tough - Regular - Easy)
(B) 30% - 60% - 90%
(C) 40% - 60% - 80%
(D) 50% - 70% - 90%

# Answer 27

**(B)** 30% - 60% - 90%

From John Dewan's Stat of the Week™, May 19, 2005: "The 30-60-90 rule of saves: Tough saves—30% conversion. Regular saves—60%. Easy saves—90%."

*Note: This is an important statistic for GMs to know when evaluating their closers. Closers with an abnormal distribution of three types of saves could be overrated or underrated, depending on the distribution, by their GMs if adjustments in the evaluation process are not made.*

## Question 28

Which is true concerning a player's defensive value versus his offensive value:

(A) his offensive value peaks before his defensive value peaks
(B) his defensive value peaks before his offensive value peaks
(C) a player's offensive and defensive value peak at the same time
(D) I don't understand these questions. When do we get to the part with the swimsuit models?

## Answer 28

**(B)** his defensive value peaks before his offensive value peaks

From *Win Shares:* "There are a lot of guys in their mid-thirties who can still hit, but who are no longer able to play the field as they once could....The answer is that defensive value *does* peak earlier than hitting value, and defensive value does account for a larger percentage of the player's value when he is young than when he is older...."

## Question 29

What happens after a batter hits a home run:

(A) batting average drops
(B) home runs go up
(C) hit batsmen and walks go up
(D) all of the above

## Answer 29

**(D)** all of the above

From the *1993 Baseball Scoreboard:* "Based on 1989 data, five things: (1) batting average for the next hitter drops about 10 points; (2) the home run rate for the next batter goes up about 10 percent; (3) the HBP rate skyrockets, 50 percent in the NL, 100 percent in the AL; (4) the base on balls rate goes up significantly; and (5) the strikeout rate rises significantly. Conclusions: about what you would expect. The pitcher is mad, and so is likely to throw a little harder and a little wilder...."

## Question 30

A player who is an average hitter in AAA ball will be what in the majors:

(A) average
(B) 8% below average
(C) 18% below average
(D) 28% below average

# Answer 30

**(C)** 18% below average

From the *1985 Baseball Abstract:* "Members of the media prefer to believe that minor league batting statistics are meaningless because it creates a mystique about major league performance....Nonetheless, it is false. Because if it was true, you wouldn't be able to project what a player will hit in the major leagues, based on what he has done in the minors. And you can....[A] player who is an average hitter in AAA ball will be about 18% below average in the majors."

*Note: Adjustments for league and home parks must be made.*

## Question 31

Two rookie hitters play the same position and have identical averages (batting average, slugging percentage, and on-base percentage). In general, which player will improve the most:

(A) the player with the most major league at-bats
(B) the younger player
(C) the player with the least major league at-bats
(D) the older player

# Answer 31

**(B)** the younger player

Conclusion from a study in the *1987 Baseball Abstract*: "A 20 year old player can be expected to play about 26% more major league games than a comparable 21 year old, 60% more than a comparable 22 year old, about twice as many as a comparable 23 year old, 2.5 times as many as a comparable 24 year old, about 2.8 times as many as a comparable 25 year old, 3.2 times as many as a comparable 26 year old, 3.7 times as many as a comparable 27 year old, and 4.3 times as many as a comparable 28 year old." Why? "Because the ability to grow in value declines with age, the extra year of growth that he gains will be a year in which he gains more than in any other year."

## Question 32

Announcers will often expound upon the virtues of moving runners with outs, i.e. hitting behind the runners, hitting sacrifice flys, etc., as opposed to making an out by striking out. How many runs are actually lost per every 100 strikeouts as opposed to 100 non-strikeout outs:

(A) 1 – 5
(B) 6 – 10
(C) 11 – 15
(D) 16 – 20

# Answer 32

**(A)** 1 – 5

Conclusion from a study in the *1986 Baseball Abstract*:"[T]he difference between 13,000 strikeouts and 13,000 ordinary outs is about 136 runs–or one run per 100 outs." James has recently revised his Runs Created Formula (see *The Bill James Handbook*). Based on his revised formula, it appears that he now estimates strikeouts as a loss of 3.3 runs per 100 strikeouts.

## Question 33

The correlation between winning a division title and leading the league in which category is the weakest:

(A) home runs
(B) batting average
(C) stolen bases
(D) walks

# Answer 33

**(C)** stolen bases

From the *1983 Baseball Abstract*: "[T]eams leading the league in stolen bases, even in this 'speed era,' [1969-1982] have done worse than teams leading the league in any other major offensive category....[T]eams finishing last in the league in stolen bases and triples are able to win far more consistently than teams finishing last in any other category.... It makes sense, don't you think, that the more important an offensive category is, the greater would be the average distance between the teams doing well in that category, and the teams doing poorly?" The distance, as far as place in the standings within a division between leading the league in a category and finishing last in a category are as follows: batting average (2.93); home runs (1.96); walks (1.81); and stolen bases (0.70). For example, the average team leading the league in stolen bases will finish less than one place (0.70) in the standings ahead of the average team last in the league in stolen bases.

## Question 34

Former manager Pete Rose once said that he didn't care what a player did last week, he only cared what the player did in his last 500 at-bats. In separate interviews, former GMs Dallas Green and Steve Phillips both stated that the worst time to make player judgements are spring training and September call-ups. No doubt, judgements made using small amounts of data are dangerous. In fact, past research has shown that spring training doesn't reveal much about the regular season with one exception. That exception is:

(A) a hitter who played winter ball the year before
(B) a hitter who will become a free agent at the end of the season
(C) a hitter who has a tremendous spring training
(D) a hitter who has recently testified before Congress

## Answer 34

**(C)** a hitter who has a tremendous spring training

From John Dewan's Stat of the Week™, March 30, 2005: "A hitter that has a tremendous spring training does correlate to a better than normal season. In precise statistical terms, a hitter with a positive difference between their spring training slugging percentage and their lifetime slugging percentage of .200 or more alerts us to a step forward in the coming season."

## Question 35

The type of pitchers who derive the most benefit in terms of ERA from night games are pitchers:

    (A) who have good control
    (B) who are groundball pitchers (balls don't get lost in the lights)
    (C) who have high ratios of both strikeouts and walks per game
    (D) who missed curfew the night before

## Answer 35

**(C)** who have high ratios of both strikeouts and walks per game

From a study in the *1984 Baseball Abstract*: Pitchers with high strikeouts and high walk totals are almost a full run (0.95) better at night than they are during the day. James states in part, "[I]n stat analysis, a run a game is a whale among minnows."

## Question 36

In 2004, the Boston Red Sox came back to beat the Yankees in the ALCS after being down three games to zero. Assuming that the Red Sox and Yankees were two even teams, what was the mathematical chance that the Red Sox would come back?

(A) 1.75 %
(B) 3.50 %
(C) 6.25 %
(D) 9.00 %

## Answer 36

**(C)** 6.25 %

From John Dewan's Stat of the Week™, October 20, 2004: "The chance of winning any game between equally matched teams is 50%, making the probability of three wins in a row .5 x .5 x .5 = .125…." Thus, four wins in a row would be .125 x .5 or 6.25%.

## Question 37

Which free-agent strategy works best:

(A) sign to "fill a need"
(B) sign the "best free agent" on the market
(C) "whole-scale" signing
(D) let all your players become free agents and then blame your 100 loss season on the size of your market

## Answer 37

**(B)** Sign the "best free agent" on the market

From the *1984 Baseball Abstract*: "[T]he best free-agent strategy approach…ignore the needs of your team, ignore the strengths and weaknesses of the players available. Just identify the best player out there, and go after him." As far as "fill a need" goes: "Whenever you talk yourself into thinking that you *need* a player that's when you pay too much for him." From the *1993 Baseball Ratings Book*: "The truth is that *all* of the teams which have adopted signing whole-scale free agents as a method of building a team have destroyed themselves."

## Question 38

Earl Weaver, manager of the Baltimore Orioles in the 1960s and 70s, once said, "[W]hen you employ one run strategies, that's all you'll get—one run." That is why, normally, one run strategies should only be used late in a game when one run becomes critical. Name four one run strategies.

## Answer 38

There are actually six one run strategies:

1. sacrifice bunts
2. intentional walks
3. stolen bases
4. guard the lines
5. pitch outs
6. infield in

## Question 39

Rank the following positions in terms of the normal average offensive output per season for each position (rank 1-8 with 1 being the best offensive position):

| | | | |
|---|---|---|---|
| First Base | _____ | Catcher | _____ |
| Second Base | _____ | Left field | _____ |
| Shortstop | _____ | Center field | _____ |
| Third Base | _____ | Right field | _____ |

## Answer 39

| | | | |
|---|---|---|---|
| First Base | 1 | Catcher | 8 |
| Second Base | 6 | Left field | 2 or 3 |
| Shortstop | 7 | Center field | 5 |
| Third Base | 4 | Right field | 2 or 3 |

## Question 40

Rank the following positions in terms of their draft rate of return (based on the drafts from 1965-1988) (rank 1-7 with 1 being the best rate of return):

First Base _____          Catcher _____
Second Base _____         Outfield _____
Shortstop _____           Pitchers _____
Third Base _____

## Answer 40

| | | | |
|---|---|---|---|
| First Base | 3 (1.02) | Catcher | 5 (0.96) |
| Second Base | 7 (0.05) | Outfield | 1 (1.24) |
| Shortstop | 4 (1.01) | Pitchers | 6 (0.88) |
| Third Base | 2 (1.16) | | |

## Question 41

True or False: Slugging percentage is a better indicator of a full-time player's value than his RBI total.

## Answer 41

**True**

Conclusion from a study in the *1987 Baseball Abstract*: RBI are "more subject to illusions of context." This means that the ability of a player's teammates to reach base has a major impact on the number of RBI available to that player. Conversely, slugging percentage, in theory, is independent of other players.

## Question 42

True or False: In general, good teams have a better win/loss percentage in their one-run games than in their non-one-run games.

## Answer 42

**False**

From the *1986 Baseball Abstract*: "[O]ne run games are *not* an indicator of a team's quality.…[T]he smaller the margin of victory, the more likely it is that the better team will lose. And, in fact,… .600 teams do not play .600 ball in one-run games, but rather something more [like] .540 ball, while .400 teams tend to move up to something like .460."

## Question 43

True or False: A shortstop worth 60 runs offensively is more valuable than a left fielder worth 70 runs offensively.

## Answer 43

**True**

From Bill James *1995 Players' Rating Book*:"A player's offensive
contribution can only be evaluated in the context of his defensive
contribution, and vice versa. A shortstop who puts 60 runs on the
scoreboard is worth more than a left fielder who creates 75 runs."The key
here is the average offensive value of a shortstop versus a left fielder.

## Question 44

True or False: It is generally better to make a 1-for-3 trade as opposed to a 3-for-1 trade.

# Answer 44

**False**

From the *1988 Baseball Abstract*: "Talent in baseball is not normally distributed. It is a pyramid. For every player who is 10 percent above the average player, there are probably 20 players who are 10 percent below average." In other words, the better the player, the harder it is to find a replacement for him; the weaker the player, the easier it is to find a replacement for him. Thus, in a 1-for-3 trade, the "1" is hard to replace and the "3's" are probably replaceable. Thus, we can make two general conclusions: (1) never trade quality for quantity; and (2) the team receiving the "best player" in a trade is the team that usually "wins" the trade.

## Question 45

True or False: The average normal platoon difference for hitters is 24 points in batting average, 53 points in slugging percentage, and 34 points in on-base percentage.

## Answer 45

**True**

The statistics are from a *1988 Baseball Abstract* study: "[T]he platoon differential is not a 'weakness' peculiar to some types of players, but is simply a condition of the game; almost every hitter and every type of hitter hits better over a period of time with than against the platoon advantage...."

## Question 46

True or False: There is a positive correlation between runs scored and temperature.

# Answer 46

**True**

From the *1993 Baseball Scoreboard*:"'Heat equals hitting.' STATS records the temperatures of every game, and from 1987 through 1989 the data showed a significant impact of weather on offense. When the temperature was above 90, there were an average of 9.1 runs and 1.83 home runs per game. When the temperature was below 60, there were 8 runs and 1.40 home runs per game."

## Question 47

True or False: In the leadoff spot, stolen bases are more important than on-base percentage.

# Answer 47

## False

From the *1998 Baseball Scoreboard*: "Since a leadoff man's primary function is to score runs, it's only natural that his most important job is to get on base." The bottom line here is that you can't steal first base.

For those of you who are interested, the formula found in the answer to Question 89 on this test can be used to verify this answer. Just take pairs of players with the same number of plate appearances, one with a higher OB and one with more stolen bases. Plug them into the formula—the high on-base player will be found to score more runs, except in extreme cases.

## Question 48

True or False: A player's minor league performance, adjusted for ballparks, leagues and levels, is a reliable indicator of major league performance.

## Answer 48

**True**

From *This Time Let's Not Eat the Bones*: "[I]f you take the time and the trouble to adjust for the illusions of minor league parks, and if you adjust also for the better competition of the major leagues, then minor league batting statistics are a perfectly reliable indicator of a player's hitting ability.... [M]inor league stats are exactly as reliable as a guide to future major league performance as are previous major league stats."

## Question 49

True or False: On-base percentage is a better indicator of a player's value than batting average.

## Answer 49

**True**

From the *1987 Baseball Abstract*: "For a hitter, there are two statistics that stand above the others. Those are on-base percentage and slugging percentage." In the simplest terms, a pitcher's job is to get the batter out. The batter's job is to not make an out and reach first base safely. On-base percentage measures the batter's ability to do his primary job.

## Question 50

True or False: The theory of supply and demand suggests that when the number of free agents increase, the average salary of free agents will decrease.

# Answer 50

**True**

Back in the 1970s when the owners and the players were negotiating free agency, Marvin Miller, the players' union representative, understood this concept and the owners did not. By agreeing to limits on free agency, Marvin Miller was able to set up a system designed to enable salaries to skyrocket. See the book *Lords of the Realm* by John Helyar.

## Question 51

True or False: Using an early first round draft pick on a pitcher is a smaller risk than using the pick on a hitter.

## Answer 51

**False**

From the *Bill James Baseball Abstract Newsletter, Special Issue No. 1*:
"Pitchers who have been made very high draft selection (drafted 1-10) in June drafts have done exceedingly poorly as professionals—far worse than players selected from any other position."

## Question 52

True or False: The odds of an intentionally walked batter scoring a run is greater than the odds of the next hitter (after the intentional walk) hitting into a double play.

## Answer 52

**True**

From the *1993 Baseball Scoreboard*:"In 1990…the batter intentionally walked came around to score 15 percent of the time….When an intentional walk set up a double play situation, a double play actually resulted only 13 percent of the time."

## Question 53

True or False: On average, catchers who play on teams with high strikeout staffs have more assists than catchers who play on teams with low strikeout staffs.

# Answer 53

**False**

From *Win Shares*: "[T]he catchers on low strikeout teams had an average of 85 assists per team. The catchers on high strikeout teams had an average of 73 assists per team." Why? On average, strikeout pitchers allow fewer baserunners than non-strikeout pitchers. Fewer baserunners mean fewer opportunities for a catcher to record an assist.

## Question 54

True or False: There is a negative correlation between the number of different lineups used by a manager and the number of games won by his team.

## Answer 54

**True**

From the *1995 Baseball Scoreboard*: "Generally, the clubs which used the most lineups lost; the ones who used the fewest won.... So frequent lineup changes *usually* tell us that a team is struggling...." The question here is much like the chicken or the egg: Are teams changing lineups because they are struggling, or do teams struggle because they keep changing lineups?

## Question 55

True or False: The average winning percentage for rookie managers in their first season as a manager is higher than the average winning percentage for veteran managers in their first season with a new team.

# Answer 55

**False**

From the *1994 Baseball Scoreboard* (study from 1946-1993):"The results are almost identical.... Previous managerial experience, one is led to conclude, doesn't make any difference."

## Question 56

True or False: For a manager, there is a positive correlation between the number of young players developed into full-time starters and the number of championships won.

# Answer 56

**True**

This is taken from a study on managers in the *Baseball Report Card*. At the time of the study, the best two managers in baseball at developing young players into full-time players were Dick Williams and Whitey Herzog, who won a combined 11 regular season titles. The worst was Chuck Tanner who had just one title in 19 seasons as a manager.

## Question 57

True or False: Players who were injury prone in the minors are more likely to be injury prone in the majors than players who were injury free in the minors.

## Answer 57

**True**

This one is from research done by Manager Phil Garner and Coach Tim Foli when they were with the Brewers. Recently Sig Mejdal did a study in *The Bill James Handbook 2005* which concurred with Garner and Foli. "[P]ast injuries are by far the most valuable predictor of future injury."

## Question 58

True or False: There is a positive correlation between attendance for a given game and the quality of starting pitchers pitching that day.

## Answer 58

**False**

From *This Time Let's Not Eat the Bones*: "Outstanding pitchers did not, on the whole, draw more fans per start than poor pitchers, to any detectable extent."

## Question 59

True or False: The number of putouts recorded by a third baseman doesn't bear any identifiable relationship to fielding excellence, good, bad or otherwise.

## Answer 59

**True**

From *Win Shares*: "In rating fielders, I use basically every available statistic, with one exception. The only thing I don't use, except in oblique ways, is putouts by a third baseman. Why? Because putouts by third basemen don't bear any identifiable relationship to fielding excellence, good, bad or otherwise."

## Question 60

True or False: Pitchers can induce double-play grounders.

# Answer 60

**False**

From the *1993 Baseball Scoreboard*:"It turns out that batters hit groundballs exactly one-third of the time, no matter what the situation. What's more, the style of the pitcher made no difference; neither groundball pitchers nor flyball pitchers were able to alter their normal frequencies of groundballs allowed."

## Question 61

True or False: Almost all good young pitchers with strikeout rates below 4.00 per game disappear quickly.

## Answer 61

**True**

This comes from a research study in the *Historical Baseball Abstract*:"[I]'ve been looking for a starting pitcher who could pitch consistently well with a low strikeout rate. I still haven't found one....The influence of strikeouts on a pitcher's future can be compared to the effect of height on a man's chances of playing in the NBA."

## Question 62

True or False: Almost all pitchers who have long careers start out with strikeout rates in excess of the league average.

## Answer 62

**True**

This is a quote from the same study referred to in Question 61 from the *Historical Baseball Abstract*:"[A]ll of the best starting pitchers since World War II have been above the league strikeout rate as young pitchers."

## Question 63

True or False: There is a clear relationship between the average age of a team's regulars and the probability that the team's record will improve or decline in the next season.

## Answer 63

**True**

From *This Time Let's Not Eat the Bones*:"[T]here is a clear relationship between the average age of a team's regulars and the probability that they will improve the next season." From the *1982 Baseball Abstract*:"A very young team has a 75% chance of improving from season to season; a very old team has only a 39% chance of improving, and has a 27% chance of suffering a serious decline."

## Question 64

True or False: Finesse pitchers are more durable and consistent than power pitchers.

## Answer 64

**False**

From the *1995 Bill James Player Ratings Book*: "Power pitchers are vastly more durable and more consistent than finesse pitchers. Never bet on a finesse pitcher to sustain success, even when he has it. Always bet on a power pitcher; you'll load the odds in your favor."

## Question 65

True or False: The baseball draft usually produces one superstar somewhere among the top 50 picks.

## Answer 65

**True**

From *This Time Let's Not Eat the Bones* (citing Special Issue No. 1 of the *Baseball Abstract Newsletter*). "So, basically, about one high draft pick a year yields a superstar — and your chances of finding a superstar with an unspecified #1 or #2 draft pick are about 1 in 50."

## Question 66

True or False: On the average, closers pitch worse in "non-save" situations than they do in save situations.

# Answer 66

**True**

From John Dewan's Stat of the Week™, June 23, 2005: "Over the last three-and-a-half years the top closers have posted an ERA of 2.51 when coming into the game in a save situation....This same group of closers had a respectable 3.26 ERA in non-save situations, but that's three quarters of a run higher than their ERA in save situations."

## Question 67

True or False: There is a formula that can be used to estimate the "trade value" a team has.

# Answer 67

**True**

This formula is from the *1986 Baseball Abstract*:

First find each player's trade value:
(AV-Y) * ((Y+1) * AV)/190 + (AV * Y * Y) / 13

> AV = approximate value (or Win Shares)
> Y = 24 - .6 * (a player's age)

Then add together all trade values for all of the players on that given team.

## Question 68

True or False: Guarding the lines in the late innings is only a good strategy in one-run games.

# Answer 68

**True**

From the *1993 Baseball Scoreboard*: "STATS carefully tracks the paths of all balls hit in play, so we can fairly accurately estimate how many hits are saved or lost by guarding the lines. The verdict? Guarding the line will save some doubles (important in a one-run game), but those are offset by the singles the defense gives up, and so increases the chances that multiple runs will be scored. And both effects are marginal."

## Question 69

True or False: No team last in the league in walks has ever won a World Championship.

## Answer 69

**True**

From the *2000 Baseball Scoreboard*: "Going back to 1901, the average winning percentage for teams which finished last in their league in walks was a dismal .445…. More to the point, no team—not a single one—has won a World Championship since 1900 while finishing last in its league in walks."

## Question 70

True or False: Great hitters are great at fouling off two-strike pitches.

# Answer 70

**False**

From the *2000 Baseball Scoreboard*: "All in all, there's little evidence that the great hitters possess some sort of supernatural ability to foul off two-strike pitches until they get one they like.... [I]t's not Tony Gwynn's ability to hit the ball foul that makes him a great hitter. It's his ability to hit the ball fair."

## Question 71

True or False: The elevation at which a park lies has a major impact on how many home runs will be hit there.

## Answer 71

**True**

From the *1988 Baseball Abstract*, conclusion from a study by Dick O'Brien: "[T]he higher the altitude of the park…the more home runs the team which played there would hit."

## Question 72

True or False: Teams that finish a season playing well do substantially better in the following season.

## Answer 72

**True**

The conclusion from a study in the *1986 Baseball Abstract*: "On the whole, there is an unmistakable advantage to teams which finished well. The difference is not enormous, but it is significant...."

## Question 73

True or False: Teams which improve their win/loss record in a given season are more likely to decline in terms of wins the next season.

## Answer 73

**True**

From the 1982 *Baseball Abstract*. "The Plexiglass Principle holds that all things in baseball have a powerful tendency to return to the form which they previously held….In 1980 only 5 major league teams moved in the same direction as they did in 1979….No team in the majors has 3 straight years of improvement or decline."

## Question 74

True or False: A team scores over three times as many runs in innings where their first hitter in the inning reaches base safely than they do in innings where the first batter makes an out.

# Answer 74

**True**

There have been a few studies on this one which all come up approximately the same. We will take our numbers from Chuck Waseleski and
the *1984 Baseball Abstract*. "[T]eams scored 50% of the time when they
got their leadoff men on, 16.8% of the time when they didn't.... Call up
your nearest baseball fan, right now, and ask him this question: How
many more runs will you score in an inning when you have the leadoff
man on than you do in an inning when you don't? I'll bet he says 28% or
something. The answer is 242%."

## Question 75

True or False: A batting order where a team's best hitters are spread out is more efficient than an order where the best hitters are bunched together.

## Answer 75

**False**

Here are the conclusions from a study on batting order in the *1984 Baseball Abstract*: "A 'bunched' offense is much more efficient than a spread-out offense; you receive a higher return on your opportunities.... The more [the] offense is bunched together, the more efficient."

## Question 76

True or False: For pitchers, there is very little relationship between success as a rookie and long term greatness.

## Answer 76

**True**

Conclusion from a study in the *1987 Baseball Abstract*: "For a pitcher, there is virtually no relationship between outstanding performance as a rookie and eventually attaining star status. Whereas about 35% of outstanding rookie non-pitchers will eventually go into the Hall of Fame, for pitchers the percentage is probably no higher than 10%."

## Question 77

True or False: Rookies on "bad" teams show a greater future growth than comparable rookies on "good" teams.

## Answer 77

**False**

Conclusion from a study in the *1987 Baseball Abstract*: "As a group, the rookies who played on good teams did go on to have distinctly, if not dramatically, better careers." The rookies from good teams played in 27% more games, hit 33% more home runs, and had 33% more hits than comparable rookies from bad teams.

## Question 78

True or False: Hitters with speed in general develop more and last longer than comparable hitters who lack speed.

## Answer 78

**True**

Conclusions from a study in the *1987 Baseball Abstract*: There is a "21% advantage for player[s] with young player's skills…. [S]peed is the key to the advantage of the players who have young player's skills…. Many players, perhaps most players, are driven out of the major leagues indirectly because they lose their speed…. [A]s a player loses speed as he ages, he loses the ability to play the positions (center field, shortstop, second base) at which offensive ability is scarce, and thus loses the ability to stay in the majors *without* [being a great hitter]."

## Question 79

True or False: It is better to stockpile first basemen than it is to stockpile shortstops.

# Answer 79

**False**

Two Reasons: (1) From the *1987 Baseball Abstract*: "[F]irst basemen do not play as long in the majors as outfielders of the same ability as hitters, no matter how well they hit. And shortstops who can hit, though few in number, tend to have tremendously long major league careers." Shortstops have the potential to have longer careers than first basemen. (2) From the *1982 Baseball Abstract*: "There exists a spectrum of defensive positions, left to right, which goes something like this: designated hitter, first base, left field, right field, third base, center field, second base, shortstop. Catchers don't count; they're a special case. Along this spectrum, each position makes larger defensive demands than the position before it.... As a player grows older…he tends to be shifted leftward along this spectrum.... [A]n intelligent trading strategy to fight against [the movement left on the defensive spectrum] is to allow the talent at the left end of the spectrum [first base] to take care of itself, as it will, and to worry [or acquire] the right end [shortstops]."

## Question 80

True or False: Based on the Law of Competitive Balance, it is harder to maintain a .600 ballclub than it is to take a .400 ballclub to .500.

# Answer 80

**True**

From the *1983 Baseball Abstract*: "Most of the teams which had winning records in [one season] will decline [the next season]; most of the teams which had losing records in [one season] will improve in [the next season]." Thus, the .600 teams will be "pushed" down toward .500 and the .400 teams will be pulled up to .500. "The essence of that difference is in how the two teams view the need to make changes. [The .600 team] develops a self-satisfaction which colors all of the decisions that the team needs to face." This means that a .600 team is much less likely to address and correct a "problem" than a .400 team. Consequently, the .400 team makes changes and improves and the .600 team declines.

## Question 81

Bill James' Runs Created Formula is used to estimate the offensive value of each hitter. There are three parts to the Runs Created Formula (A * B)/C. "A" is a given player's ability to get on base. "B" is a given player's ability to advance runners. What is "C?"

## Answer 81

A given player's plate appearances.

## Question 82

When evaluating hitters, the owner of your team only understands batting average. However, he has agreed to look at one more statistic for each hitter as long as it is used in conjunction with batting average. What is the name of the statistic that takes into account everything of offensive value which isn't included in batting average that you can present to your owner?

# Answer 82

Secondary Average [SA], which is an estimate of a player's offensive contributions not reflected in his batting average.

SA = [TB - H + BB + SB] / AB

| | | |
|---|---|---|
| TB | = | Total Bases |
| H | = | Hits |
| BB | = | Walks |
| SB | = | Stolen Bases |
| AB | = | At-Bats |

## Question 83

OPS is often used as a quick and dirty substitute for Runs Created per Game when a quick evaluation is needed. What is OPS?

## Answer 83

On-base percentage plus slugging percentage.

## Question 84

Your pitching coach tells you your team is going to allow 800 runs this season. Your batting coach says that your team will score 700 runs. Use the Pythagorean Formula to determine how many games you will win this season.

## Answer 84

70 games. Use the Pythagorean Theorem for Baseball:

$700^2 / (700^2 + 800^2) * 162 = 70.25$ or 70 wins.

## Question 85

All other things being equal, and based solely on the following information, who was the better defensive shortstop in 2004?

Jimmy Rollins with a fielding percentage of .986 and an adjusted range of 4.00, or Bobby Crosby with a fielding percentage of .975 and an adjusted range of 4.96.

## Answer 85

Bobby Crosby. Even though Crosby made 10 more errors than Rollins, Crosby recorded 135 more outs than Rollins in 20.7 less innings. Again, all other things being equal, Crosby is 135 outs better. From the *1982 Baseball Abstract*: "[T]he player's range afield is the most important single factor at every position except first base and catcher and possibly second...Larry Bowa in most seasons may make a half dozen errors fewer than Ozzie Smith, but Smith will make literally hundreds more plays a year than Bowa does. Every year. There is no conceivable way in which the half-dozen plays which are Bowa's advantage can be held to substantially balance the hundreds of balls that Smith will get to [which] Bowa will not." All other things being equal, go with range over fielding percentage.

## Question 86

Component ERA is the formula used to eliminate "hit element luck" from a pitcher's ERA in order to produce a more representative ERA for a given pitcher. Fill in the missing part of the following sentence: "Component ERA is the ERA that we would expect a pitcher to have given his _____, _____, _____, and _____ allowed per nine innings."

## Answer 86

From the *Historical Baseball Abstract*: walks, hits, hit batsmen, and home runs.

## Question 87

Calculate ERA for a pitcher with the following statistics: 180 innings pitched; and 90 runs allowed including 10 unearned runs allowed.

## Answer 87

4.00.

The formula: ER * 9 /IP or (90-10) * 9 / 180.

ER = earned runs
IP = innings pitched.

This should have been an easy one. Right?

## Question 88

Defensive Efficiency is a defense's ability to turn batted balls into outs. Within 5%, what is the average number of batted balls turned into outs by major league teams?

## Answer 88

From the *1987 Baseball Abstract*: "An average defensive efficiency record is about .695. Almost all successful teams will be above average." Meaning an average defensive team will turn 69.5% of batted balls in play into outs.

## Question 89

True or False: There is a formula which can be used to accurately predict the number of runs a given leadoff man will score during the season.

# Answer 89

**True**

There is a formula which can be used to accurately predict the number of runs a given leadoff man will score during the season. From the *1983 Baseball Abstract*: "What you do is, you figure the number of times the guy is likely to be on first, and you multiply that by .35. You figure how many times he is likely to be on second, and you multiply that by .55. To this you add .80 times the number of triples and 1.00 times the number of home runs the player has hit. The result gives the number of runs that he is likely to have scored, given a normal offense coming up behind him and normal clutch performance when he is on base...."

Note: Times on first equals (H+BB-XBH-SB-CS); Times on second equals (2B+SB).

| | | |
|---|---|---|
| H | = | Hits |
| BB | = | Walks |
| XBH | = | Extra Base Hits |
| SB | = | Stolen Bases |
| CS | = | Caught Stealing |
| 2B | = | Doubles |

## Question 90

In the book *Moneyball*, Oakland's GM Billy Beane stresses the importance of on-base percentage. What is the formula for on-base percentage?

## Answer 90

(Hits + Walks + Hit-by-Pitcher) / (At-bats + Walks + Hit-by-Pitcher + Sacrifice Flies)

## Question 91

**January 2005** Jeromy Burnitz is projected to hit 31 home runs for the Rockies in the 2005 season. However, Burnitz just signed with the Cubs for 2005. How many home runs should he hit for the Cubs? Key Stats: The home run index for lefties at Coors Field (Rockies) is 1.47. The home run index for lefties at Wrigley Field (Cubs) is .97.

# Answer 91

**25**

First estimate the number of home runs hit at home (H) and on the road (R):

$H + R = 31$ and $H = R * 1.47$

thus $1.47R + 1R = 31$ or $2.47R = 31$ or $R = 31/(2.47)$ or $R = 12.55$

thus $H = (31-12.55)$ or $18.45$

then neutralize the home HR: $18.45/1.47 = 12.55$

then convert to Wrigley $12.55 * .97 = 12.17$

Thus $12.55 + 12.17 = $ **24.72**

*Note: Jeromy Burnitz hit 24 home runs for the Cubs in 2005.*

## Question 92

**November 1996** Dave Burba (11-13, 3.83 ERA, IP—195, Runs allowed—101) is in contract negotiations. He maintains he didn't get any run support in 1995. He wants to know how many games he would have won with average run support (4.68 runs per a game).

## Answer 92

**12**

First calculate normal run support for 195 innings: 4.68 * 195/9 = 101.4.
Plug this number into the Pythagorean Formula to determine his win
total with normal support: Runs scored$^2$ / (runs scored$^2$ + runs allowed$^2$) *
decisions (24). Runs Scored would be 101.4. Runs allowed would be 101.
This produces 12 wins. See the article on "John Smiley's Shoes" in Part
One (page 38) of this book.

## Question 93

**November 1992** GM Sal Bando informs you that owner Bud Selig has authorized only enough money to re-sign either Robin Yount or Paul Molitor. Molitor is clearly the better hitter with the better future. Yount is the fan favorite. Do you recommend that he keep the better player or the player better loved by the fans?

# Answer 93

## Molitor

From the *1993 Player Ratings Book*: "Nothing could be more obvious than this: that the fans simply want to win. If you win, the fans will be happy." The Brewers haven't had a winning season since they let Molitor leave and kept Yount in an effort to keep Brewer fans happy. See Part One of this book for more details on the Molitor decision (page 42).

## Question 94

**Spring 1978** The San Diego Padres have two good, young shortstops in Ozzie Smith and Bill Almon. Smith wins the Padres' starting shortstop job. According to the theories behind the "Defensive Spectrum," to what position should the Padres move Almon in order to maximize his value?

# Answer 94

## Second Base

From the *1982 Baseball Abstract*: "Since shortstop is the most demanding defensive position, the position furthest to the right on the [defensive] spectrum, any movement would be a leftward movement, and thus a comparatively safe one from a defensive standpoint.... Since the right-most positions are the most difficult to fill, the sensible and natural thing to do would have been to consider Almon first as a second baseman...." What did the Padres do? Well, the Padres moved Almon three positions to the left on the defensive spectrum skipping over second base and center field to third base. Unfortunately, the move was too far left on the spectrum for Almon's bat. Almon simply couldn't hit enough to be a productive third baseman. Thus, Almon was subsequently benched.

## Question 95

**All-Star Break 2004** You are Phil Garner and you have just been hired to manage the Astros. You notice that the Astros are (-5) in Pythagorean wins, an indication that their bullpen has been very inefficient. You have a great closer in Brad Lidge. How would you use Lidge the rest of the season to maximize his impact on the Astros' win/loss record?

## Answer 95

Conclusions from a study in the *Historical Baseball Abstract*: "The very optimal usage pattern, I believe, would be to use the relief ace: two innings a game when the game is tied; two innings a game when you have a one-run lead; and one inning at a time in other games when the game is close at the end and the relief ace hasn't been used for a day or two."

*Note: See Part Three of the book to see what was done in 2004 by Astros Manager Phil Garner.*

## Question 96

**August 1, 2004** You have been hired by Phil Garner to help his struggling Astros. You notice that the Astros have scored 25 less runs than expected based on the Runs Created Formula. This indicates that their batting order is screwed up. Here is their batting order as of August 1. What is wrong with it based on their 2004 on-base percentages and their 2004 slugging percentages?

|   |         | OBP/SLG    |
|---|---------|------------|
| 1. | Biggio  | .337/.469  |
| 2. | Everett | .317/.385  |
| 3. | Beltran | .367/.548  |
| 4. | Berkman | .450/.566  |
| 5. | Kent    | .348/.531  |
| 6. | Bagwell | .377/.465  |
| 7. | Ensberg | .330/.411  |
| 8. | Ausmus  | .306/.325  |

# Answer 96

There are two main problems with this batting order:

(1) The order isn't bunched. Everett is the Astros' seventh best hitter in terms of OPS (on-base percentage + slugging percentage) and is batting second. Everett needs to be moved down to the seventh spot.

(2) Bagwell and his .377 on-base percentage is being "wasted" at the end of the bunch. Bagwell must be moved up in the order. The player with the largest split between his slugging percentage and his on-base percentage (Kent) should be at the end of the bunch.

To correct these problems, Everett was moved down to seventh and Bagwell was moved up to third. And yes, Biggio's on-base percentage is a little low for a leadoff hitter. However, Biggio will probably lead off for the Astros until Willy Taveras is ready to take over the role. See Part Three of this book for more details.

## Question 97

**Draft Day** You have a top ten draft pick. In general, who should you draft (circle one in each pair):

(A) high school or college
(B) a shortstop or second baseman
(C) great speed or great hitter
(D) pitcher or hitter

## Answer 97

(A) high school or **college** (see Question 26)
(B) a **shortstop** or second baseman (see Question 40)
(C) great speed or **great hitter**
(D) pitcher or **hitter** (see Question 51)

The answer to these questions can be found in others within this quiz listed above. The exception is "C" and it can be explained simply — a player has to be able to hit to make it in the majors. Every AL team has a DH. Teams rarely carry pinch-runners. See the book *Moneyball* for thoughts and drafting strategies on this subject by the Oakland Athletics.

## Question 98

**March 1985** Manager Pete Rose of the Cincinnati Reds named no hit, good field catcher Dann Bilardello as his starting catcher. Rose then had three choices for the righthanded hitting Bilardello's backup:

(A) Brad Gulden—a lefty batter
(B) Alan Knicely—a righty batter who was a good hitter but a weak fielder
(C) Dave Van Gorder—a righty batter who was a good fielder but a weak hitter

Pick one as your backup and explain why.

# Answer 98

**(A)** Brad Gulden—a lefty batter

or

**(B)** Alan Knicely—a righty batter who was a good hitter but a weak fielder

From the *1991 Bill James Baseball Book*: "If your two catchers do *different* things then you have opportunities to exploit an advantage or avoid a disadvantage." Catcher is the only position where there "has" to be some type of platoon or substantial resting of the starter taking place. Only one catcher in the majors caught more than 126 games in 2004. That means 29 of the 30 major league teams needed to sit their starter for at least 36 games. Back to the 1985 Reds—the two obvious choices are Gulden or Knicely. Gulden is a good choice because he is a lefty and Bilardello, the starter, is a righty. Knicely would also be a good choice because Knicely was the opposite of Bilardello, a good hit, bad field catcher. Knicely could start against the "non-base-stealing teams." What did the Reds do in 1985? They kept Van Gorder.

## Question 99

**Late August 2004** The Reds decide to dump Barry Larkin. They have two choices for the replacement shortstop: Felipe Lopez or Andy Machado. Should the Reds immediately make a decision on who should play shortstop, or should they alternate each player, giving them 20 starts each the rest of the season and make a decision based on those 20 starts?

# Answer 99

**Make a decision right away.**

Anyone is capable of looking like the next Pete Rose for 20 games. For Reds fans, the name Paul Householder comes to mind. The decision should be made based on each player's statistics over the last three seasons and based on minor league statistics. Lopez was the clear choice. Three years of statistics is a much better basis for judging players than 20 games. The only thing we can learn by the Reds' decision to play musical chairs with their shortstops Lopez and Machado over the last 40 games of the 2004 season is that Reds GM Dan O'Brien would probably not do very well on this test.

## Question 100

**1996** Owner Bud Selig wants to fire pitching coach Don Rowe. Manager Phil Garner calls you up and asks you to do a study to determine whether or not Don Rowe has done a good job. How will you go about doing such a study?

## Answer 100

Use projections from past seasons to compare how Brewer pitchers should have performed versus their actual performance over the years under pitching coach Don Rowe.

*Note: Bud Selig always liked to fire someone every offseason in an effort to give fans a reason to believe things would be different the next season. For example, one year coaches Duffy Dyer and Tim Foli were fired. One year batting coach Mike Easler was fired. In 1996, Bud was after Don Rowe. Manager Phil Garner paid me to do a study to determine whether or not Rowe should be fired. In the pitching study I concluded that Rowe should not be fired. The report only saved Rowe's job for one more season, however. Rowe was fired in 1997.*

## The Grading Scale

| | |
|---|---|
| 90-100 correct: | Major League GM |
| 80-89 correct: | Major League Manager |
| 70-79 correct: | Major League Coach |
| 60-69 correct: | Minor League Manager |
| less than 60 correct: | Girlie Man |

Part Three

# CASE STUDY: THE HOUSTON ASTROS' 2004 RUN FOR THE PENNANT

# August 1 - October 21, 2004

On, August 1, 2004, the Houston Astros were 52-52 overall, and 8-8 under interim manager Phil Garner.

Having worked with Phil Garner in Milwaukee, I thought I would do a little research on the Astros. I had enjoyed working with him there and thought it could be fun to do again. The harder I looked at the Astros, the more confident I became that I could help the team make it to the playoffs. I decided to give Phil Garner a call.

Garner and I spent a few minutes getting caught up and then our talk turned to the Astros. Garner told me that even though the Astros were his hometown team, being a Houston resident since his playing days, he wasn't sure that he wanted to take the Astros' job. Two and a half months is a very short time to turn things around. He was concerned that if he failed to make a significant difference, he would never get another opportunity to manage in the majors. On the other hand, if he didn't take the job, he might never get another opportunity to manage in the majors either.

As it happened, once the Astros moved into contention it came out in the press that a number of GMs had Phil Garner at or near the top of their lists before the Astros hired him. This was news to Garner.

Of course, Garner did wind up accepting the job. He couldn't just sit by and let what might be his last opportunity slip right past him.

As we spoke on the phone, it became clear that Garner had some hesitation on hiring me as a consultant: "Well, Doug," he said to me, "there are a lot of teams now doing the things you used to do for us [in Milwaukee]. There are a lot of baseball teams who now put great value on statistical analysis. Unfortunately, the Astros are not one of them. Gerry Hunsicker [Astros GM] will give it lip service from time to time. However, he really doesn't use it to any extent."

Well, I knew what that meant. Phil was only the interim manager. He didn't have the clout to get me on the payroll, nor did he want to risk trying. If Hunsicker did not put a lot of credence in statistics, Hunsicker might not put a lot of credence in a manager who did.

I told Garner I wanted to help out anyway, and made the three recommendations listed below. The logic behind these recommendations will be explained in the following stories.

1.  Promote pitcher Brandon Backe and remove Tim Redding from the rotation.
    See dates 8/3, 8/21.
2.  Tweak the batting order.
    See dates 8/1, 8/5, 8/6, 8/11, 8/15.
3.  Acquire a catcher.
    See dates 8/4, 8/19, 8/25.

The Astros did make the first two changes. Backe would pitch extremely well for the Astros and the batting order changes would be sighted by announcers/ ex-players Rick Sutcliffe and Joe Morgan as the turning point in the Astros' season. As for the Astros, who were 52-52 on this day, they would go 40-18 over the last 58 games, including a white hot 36-10 finish—the best finish for any National League team since the early fifties. This enabled the Astros to leap frog over five teams and steal the NL wild card playoff spot. The Astros continued on and won their first postseason series in Houston Astros history.

To follow are 22 behind-the-scenes stories from the Astros' improbable 2004 run for the National League Wild Card.

# Batting Order

**8/1/04:** There were two problems with the Astros' batting order: (1) The Astros' order was not bunched. Statistical studies have shown that a batting order where a team's best hitters are bunched together at the top of the order produces more runs than orders that are not bunched. The key hitter to a bunched order is the number two hitter. The correlation between total team runs and the number two spot in the order is stronger than any other spot in the order. If a team's number two hitter scores a lot of runs, then his team scores a lot of runs. (2) The Astros had a couple of their best slugging percentage hitters (batters who drive in runs) batting ahead of a couple of their best on-base percentage hitters (batters who get on base and score runs). A batting order produces more runs when a batting order's RBI men bat after the players who get on base.

In an effort to avoid whole scale order changes, I first recommended just one small change—switch Lance Berkman, the Astros' best on-base percentage hitter who was currently batting fourth, with Carlos Beltran, the Astros' best slugging percentage hitter who was currently batting third. Manager Phil Garner responded that that was one of the first things he looked at when he took over this club. Phil, however, talked to a reliable source in Kansas City who told him not to bat Beltran fourth, that Beltran simply wasn't comfortable being the order's main RBI man.

Studies concerning whether or not a given player bats better in one spot in the order than another have been inconclusive and, furthermore, any difference in performances appear, for the most part, to be simply a result of random fluctuations. This means that Beltran was a major league hitter. He could handle pressure or he wouldn't be in the majors in the first place. However, I thought I would look up the numbers anyway. Beltran's lifetime slugging percentage out of the four-spot was .065 lower than that of his numbers out of the three-spot. Yes, there was a difference in Beltran's slugging percentage, but not a large enough difference to prove that Beltran couldn't hit fourth. I e-mailed the numbers to Phil. I stated that I would still recommend switching Beltran and Berkman. However, given the numbers and the warning from Kansas City, I knew the Beltran/Berkman switch would not happen now. Thus, we would have to come up with some alternative batting order changes.

**8/5/04:** The Astros left 12 men on base in a very painful loss to the Braves. The batting order had to be changed so the Astros would start driving in runners instead of leaving them on base. Here are the highlights from the e-mail I sent

Phil the next morning concerning recommended changes to the Astros' batting order.

1. The most efficient batting order is a "bunched" order, where a team's best five hitters are all "bunched" at the top of the batting order. The Astros' five best hitting starters this season have been: Berkman; Beltran; Bagwell; Biggio; and Kent. Last night is a perfect example of what happens when a "weaker" hitter, Everett, is stuck in the middle of your five best hitters. Your team leaves a lot of baserunners on base. The Astros' batting order needs to be "bunched" with their five best hitters "bunched" at the top of the order.

2. A team's best on-base percentage hitters should always bat ahead of a team's best slugging percentage hitters. In 20 of the major league teams, the same hitter leads his team in both on-base percentage and slugging percentage. In 8 of the other 10 teams, the player leading the team in slugging percentage is batting lower in the order than the on-base percentage leader. The two exceptions are the Yankees where their leading on-base percentage player is a slow footed catcher, Posada, and the Astros, where Berkman, the best on-base hitter, bats after Beltran, the team's best slugging percentage player. Berkman needs to bat in front of Beltran and Bagwell needs to bat in front of Kent. Like in the case of Berkman and Beltran, Bagwell has the good on-base percentage and Kent has the good slugging percentage.

**8/6/04**: Phil used the batting order I recommended this game: 1-Biggio; 2-Berkman; 3-Beltran; 4-Bagwell; 5-Kent; 6-Ensberg; 7-Everett; 8-Catcher. The order did what it was supposed to do—produce runs at the top of the order with each of the first four batters scoring a run. Announcer and former pitcher Rick Sutcliffe would later state that this batting order change to move Bagwell up from the sixth spot into the middle of the order was the change that turned the Astros' season around.

Here is a quote from an August 6, 2004, *Houston Chronicle* article concerning the batting order changes: "Garner wants to see if putting his players with higher on-base percentages near the top of the order will help run production." "For a number of years, there have been a lot of studies," Garner said. "Sabermetricians have been working on this…and I've actually toyed with it on a number of occasions. I don't know if I believe it to the letter, but I practice it. I like high on-base percentage guys at the top of the lineup because they're going to be the ones who get on base and give your slugging guys a chance to drive in runs."

Bunching the order was never mentioned in the *Chronicle* article as one of the reasons for the batting order change. This is because in order to explain bunching, Phil would have had to explain that Everett was not one of the Astros' best hitters. One of the things a good manager doesn't do is criticize his players in the press. Thus, Phil only cited the positive reasons for the batting order change. Phil would tell me later, while it was a necessary change to bunch the order, he could see why it was so tempting for managers to bat someone with good bat control like Everett at the top of the order. Everett could do many different things to advance runners when the Astros were finding it difficult to score runs. Hitting behind a runner and scoring one run in the first inning is good. Hitting a double and scoring several runs in the first inning is better.

**8/10/04**: It had now been four games since the batting order change and the Astros were 1-3 with the new order. In the last two games, the top of the order, Biggio and Berkman, were on base eight times. However, the Astros lost both games as Carlos Beltran followed Biggio and Berkman by going 0-for-7 while hitting into two double plays. Overall, for the four games since the batting order change, Biggio and Berkman reached base 14 times. Beltran, however, followed them by going 2-for-14 with no RBI. The first two hitters in the order were constantly on base, but the third batter, the one with the highest slugging percentage, just wasn't producing.

Four games is simply too small a sample to draw any valid conclusions. However, let's review what we have here: Beltran should be a great RBI man because he has a high slugging percentage and doesn't walk often. I suggested that he bat fourth behind Berkman, but Phil's Kansas City friend warned him not to put Beltran in that slot. I then recommended that we rearrange the batting order so that the third batter became the key RBI spot in the order by sticking Berkman in the number two slot. This way Beltran would be the Astros' key RBI hitter, but not bat fourth. The result: Beltran quit hitting. Was this just a coincidence? I think so, but the season was slipping away from the Astros and there was cause for concern. The question now was how patient would Phil be with Beltran in the number three spot.

**8/11/04**: Phil did tweak the batting order for this game by dropping Berkman, who prefers to bat fourth anyway, down to the number four slot. This moved Beltran and Bagwell up one notch each in the order. This also moved the struggling Beltran out of the key RBI slots in the order. This batting order change was able to work for the following reasons: (1) the Astros' batting order remained bunched with the Astros' top five hitters at the top of the order; (2) Jeff Kent, a high slugging percentage, RBI hitter, was still at the end of the bunch; and (3) Beltran caught fire in the number two slot. Ten-and-a-half times in the Astros' last thirty-seven wins Beltran had the Astros' best offensive game (best "net"). No other Astro had more than 4.5 best offensive games or nets the rest of the season. Nets = (times on-base + total bases + sacrifices + stolen bases - outs used) for a given game. Hall of Famer Joe Morgan who batted third for the World Champion Reds in 1975 and 1976, the same years he won his two MVP awards, stated that the turning point in the Astros' season was when the Astros moved Beltran out of the third spot in the order.

Phil's reasoning to the press for this change in the order was that sometimes you just need to put the guys where they are the most comfortable. Phil's statement put the focus on Berkman and protected the struggling Beltran. Berkman, by the way, was great in the number two slot reaching base safely 10 of his 16 at-bats with a home run.

This batting order (Biggio, Beltran, Bagwell, Berkman, Kent, Ensberg, Vizcaino, and Ausmus) would stay in place the rest of the season.

# True Performance ERA and Brandon Backe

**8/3/04:** I sent Phil a fax on the Astros' "True Performance ERAs." This was research I used to recommend to Phil that the Astros recall Brandon Backe and remove Tim Redding from their rotation.

True Performance ERA is a pitcher's ERA minus the good or bad luck which can skew his ERA. There are two types of ERA luck:

Hit Element Luck: This luck has to do with the timing of the "elements" (hits, walks, home runs, etc.) a pitcher allows. For most pitchers, a pitcher's ERA can be estimated fairly accurately by his elements allowed. Studies have indicated that differences between a pitcher's calculated ERA based on his elements and actual ERA are random fluctuations or simply a result of good or bad luck. Relief pitchers often have a large element fluctuation in their ERA because of the smaller number of innings they pitch and the fact that they enter games in mid-innings. What is great about True Performance ERA is that it can eliminate such problems and give an accurate ERA for all pitchers, including relief pitchers.

Defensive Luck: Recently Voris McCracken conducted an important study which concluded that, other than getting strikeouts and allowing home runs, there is little a pitcher can do to cause his hits allowed to be higher or lower. Thus, in theory, pitchers are only responsible for walks, strikeouts, hit batters, and home runs. And, also in theory, all pitchers on a given pitching staff should give up approximately the same number of hits per batted balls in play. Therefore differences between a pitcher's actual percentage of hits to balls in play and the team average are considered to be the result or either good or bad luck, or good or bad defense. I suggest that anyone who is interested in more information on McCracken's study read Bill James' *Historical Baseball Abstract*.

How do we eliminate good and bad luck and find True Performance ERA?

To eliminate Element Luck we can use Bill James' Component ERA Formula which can be found in *The Bill James Handbook 2006* or in James' *Win Shares* book. The Handbook also lists the Component ERA each season for all pitchers currently in the majors. The Component ERA Formula produces the ERA which we would expect a pitcher to have given his walks, hits, hit batsmen, and home runs allowed per nine innings.

To eliminate Defensive Luck we simply calculate a given teams' percentage of defensive hits allowed per balls hit in play. Then, take that percentage and multiply it by a pitcher's batted balls in play to produce his expected hits allowed.

And then substitute the expected hits allowed total for his actual hits in James' Component ERA Formula and recalculate. This produces his True Performance ERA. Now there are some adjustments that have to be made and I have simplified things a bit. I'm assuming at this point that anyone who is really interested in this sort of calculation already owns a copy of one of James' books and can figure things out from here.

As recommended, Phil removed Tim Redding from the Astros' rotation immediately. Redding only started one more game for the Astros all season—a result of a September doubleheader. One factor which I am sure contributed to the removal of Redding from the Astros' rotation was the fact that in an emergency start the week before, Darren Oliver was pulled from the bullpen and pitched five shutout innings. Thus, if Phil Garner wanted to keep Oliver in the rotation, he needed to drop one starter from the rotation and the low man according to the True Performance ERA was Redding. When I talked to Phil on August 1 about yanking Redding, Phil told me that Redding had major league stuff, but he had problems with his pitching scheme, i.e. his approach to hitters.

However, Brandon Backe was not recalled. When I talked to Phil on August 1 about Backe, Phil stated that the Astros did indeed like Backe, but obviously not enough to recall him at this time.

**8/18/04:** The Astros announced that their ace (in terms of games won last season) Andy Pettitte was out for the rest of the season. The Astros had now lost 21-game winner (in 2003) Andy Pettitte, 14-game winner (in 2003) Wade Miller, and their starting shortstop, Adam Everett. Every team has injuries, but losing two of your top four starting pitchers is hard to overcome. In fact, the argument could be made that if Pettitte stayed healthy, the Astros would have beaten the Cardinals in the NLCS. The good news was that help was on the way in the form of a fifth "Killer B"—Brandon Backe, who was recalled to take Pettitte's place on the roster.

**8/21/04:** This was a turning point for both the Astros and the Cubs. For the Astros, Brandon Backe was recalled and pitched a heck of a good game. Backe brought with him an "I don't care who I pitch against, I expect to win" attitude that the Astros needed. And it appeared to be contagious because the Astros, after blowing a lead in the top of the ninth, came back and won the game with two runs in the bottom of the ninth. This loss was also key for the Cubs, because it cast doubt over the Cubs' bullpen. The Cubs' closer, LaTroy Hawkins, would struggle the remainder of the season, giving the Cubs a real blow in the confidence department. Conversely, the Astros' closer Brad Lidge would pick it up after this rough outing and be practically unhittable the rest of the season.

# Catchers

**8/4/04:** The third recommendation I made to Phil Garner on August 1 was concerning the Astros' backup catcher. The ideal situation for any position is to have a backup with different strengths than the starter. This way a manager can use days off to take advantage of a tough pitching matchup for the starting player. The most common starter/backup combination is the lefty/righty situation. For example, the Astros' start all righties in their infield and their backups are all lefties with Mike Lamb at 3b and 1b and Jose Vizcaino (a switch-hitter) at 2b and SS. There are other starter/backup combinations such as good hit/good field or even single hitter/power hitter. The Astros' problem at catcher was that they had two good field/no hit, righthanded batting catchers—Brad Ausmus and Raul Chavez. There is no way to platoon these guys and take advantage of their strengths or protect their weaknesses. Phil Garner did the only thing he could do, which was to assign pitchers to the catchers and pinch-hit for the catchers late in the game. The problem with this strategy is that it shortens an already short Astros' bench. The team carried 12 pitchers, leaving 13 hitters. Having to use a pinch-hitter for their catcher each game and then having to insert the backup catcher left the Astros with only three other available bench players each game. Phil was in agreement with me on this catching problem and asked me to find either a lefty catcher or a better offensive righty catcher.

In retrospect, how bad were the Astros' catchers in 2004? There were 20 catchers in the majors in 2004 who had 100 or more starts. The worst hitting catcher among the 20 in terms of OPS (on-base percentage plus slugging percentage) was the Astros' starting catcher Brad Ausmus, with a paltry OPS of .631. Why did Ausmus start so many games with such a weak bat? Ausmus' backup Raul Chavez had a meager OPS of just .515 for the 2004 season.

Bill James devised Win Shares to reduce a player's statistics to a single number related to the number of wins he contributed to his team. It includes offensive, pitching and defensive accomplishments. A Win Share is one-third of a team's win, credited to an individual player. The Win Shares credited to the players on a team always total up to exactly three times the team's win total for the season.

There are several fun and practical uses for Win Shares. Uncovering a weak position is one use. This is done by grouping a team's hitters by the position where they played the most innings and to see what the team Win Share total is for each position. For the Astros, it broke down like this:

| | |
|---|---|
| **RF-32** | Berkman (32) |
| **CF-27** | Beltran (17), Lane*(6), Hidalgo*(4) |
| **2B-24** | Kent (24) |
| **1B-23** | Bagwell (23) |
| **LF-22** | Biggio (18), Palmeiro (4) |
| **3B-22** | Lamb (12), Ensberg (10) |
| **SS-20** | Everett (10), Vizcaino (8), Bruntlett (2) |
| **C-7** | Ausmus (6), Chavez (1) |

Add 97 for the Astro pitchers for a team total of 276 Win Shares or 92 wins. The catcher position was almost three times worse than the Astros' second lowest position. To demonstrate just how bad things were at catcher for the Astros in 2004, if all eight of the Astros' everyday positions had a total of seven Win Shares each, the Astros would have won just 51 games in 2004.

*Lane and Hidalgo are listed in center due to the outfield position changes by the starters when Beltran was acquired.

**8/14/04** Catchers are not able to catch every day. In fact, only one catcher in Major League baseball in 2004 started more than 126 games (Jason Kendall—145). The Astros needed to get at least 36 starts out of their backup catcher and, given the fact that the Astros' starting catcher Brad Ausmus was 35 years old, we should probably bump that up to about 40 to 42 starts from their backup. Since Ausmus and backup Raul Chavez were similar players, there was no good way to platoon the two. Phil's best option was to select a pitcher for Chavez to catch. That pitcher was Roy Oswalt, who started 35 games. Phil still needed a few more starts out of Chavez, so when Carlos Hernandez was recalled Chavez was also assigned to Hernandez. Chavez would now catch both Oswalt and Hernandez the rest of the season.

## Todd Pratt

**8/19/04:** Sometimes timing is everything. Phil was looking for an upgrade at catcher and I was asked to find either a lefty hitting catcher or good hitting catcher.

To evaluate possible catching acquisitions, I purchased a disk containing the 2004 offensive projections for major league and AAA hitters from Diamond

Mind Baseball. Using the information on the projection disk, I made a list of 20 catchers who were currently not starting in the majors who would be an offensive upgrade for the Astros. By putting together this list, I could see which teams valued projections and statistics. The Athletics, Blue Jays and Red Sox all had two catchers in the top 12 on my list, meaning that these three teams all had three catchers each who were all better hitters than the Astros' starting catcher Brad Ausmus. I put these 20 catchers on a list in order of their 2004 offensive projections, beginning with the catcher who was projected to be the best hitter. The best offensively projected, non-starting catcher was 37-year-old Todd Pratt on the Philadelphia Phillies. Pratt actually had a career on-base percentage better than Beltran or Kent coming into the 2004 season. I faxed off this list to Phil before the game against the Phillies on August 19. Pratt started this game and went 0-5, including grounding into a key triple play with the bases loaded. The next day Phil sent me an e-mail that stated simply: "Pratt is not the answer!" A couple weeks later we discussed the catching list and Phil told me that he had only seen Pratt play a few times in his career. Perhaps Pratt was a good player, but every time he saw Pratt play the guy was terrible. He added that there is a tendency to doubt the credibility of the projections when the guy who is projected to be the best hitter is someone who you think is a poor player (or when that someone goes 0-for-5 and grounds into a triple play with the bases loaded in a key situation). Again, timing is everything. If Pratt had gone 3-for-5, the Astros might have gone out and acquired a catcher from my list. Maybe.

**8/25/04:** Todd Pratt update: Pratt started for the Phillies on August 25 against the Astros. Phil Garner had stated that every time he sees Pratt, Pratt stinks. Well, he did it again by ending four different innings with an out in four separate at-bats. This is really a hard feat to accomplish. Pratt struck out to end the second, struck out to end the fourth; grounded out to end the sixth; and flew out to end the eighth. Pratt should just ask manager Larry Bowa not to play him when Phil Garner is around.

## Jason Kendall

**8/25/04:** Speaking of possible catchers to acquire, earlier in the day, Phil asked me to give him my assessment of Pirate Catcher Jason Kendall. Astros GM Gerry

Hunsicker had told Phil that the Pirates were offering Kendall in a possible trade with the Astros. Jason Kendall would be a giant step up from the Astros' current catching situation. We discussed Kendall's defense briefly. His throwing at one time was a little suspect. In 2004, however, Kendall led the majors in catching assists and was third best among starting catchers in caught stealing percentage (.32). Also, I always try to give Phil something non-statistical about the player in question that I know would be important to Phil. In Kendall's case, I pointed out that earlier this season when playing a doubleheader in an American League park, Kendall caught both games back-to-back. Most good hitting catchers such as Kendall would have caught the first game and then been the designated hitter for the second game. Catching both games of a doubleheader is the kind of toughness that Phil Garner loves. For the year, Kendall started 145 games, which was 19 more games than anyone else in the majors in 2004. Now, the Astros never did trade for Kendall. So, do you think Phil changed his mind and told Gerry, no I don't want All-Star, assist leader, catch-both-ends-of-a-doubleheader, tough guy Jason Kendall. I want that Todd Pratt guy. Yeah, maybe.

**8/30/04:** We were just one day away from the last day a player may be acquired and still be eligible for the playoff roster. The two Astros' catchers, Ausmus and Chavez, combined for seven hits in the last three days. It didn't look like there would be any changes at catcher.

## Brad Ausmus

**9/18/04:** In the sixth, Beltran threw out yet another Brewer at the plate. The collision on the play at the plate resulted in a concussion for Brad Ausmus. Despite the concussion, not only did Ausmus hang on for the out, but he batted one more time before leaving the game.

After the collision, the Astros' medical staff asked Ausmus a few questions, such as: "What is the score?"; "Who are we playing?"; and "What inning is it?" Ausmus had no idea, but like a second grader finding answers to a spelling test on the blackboard, Ausmus found the answers on the scoreboard and managed to answer the questions correctly. However, after a subsequent at-bat where Ausmus looked as lost as a second grader on the first day at a new school, the gig was up and Ausmus was removed from the game and sent to the hospital.

## Mike Matheny

**9/28/04:** Statistically, one of the hardest things to evaluate is a catcher's ability to handle a pitching staff.* Yes, in some cases a catcher's ERA (the ERA for pitchers while a given catcher is catching) can be used, but in many cases, because of the way the catchers are used, catcher's ERA is not very meaningful. Phil Garner grabbed Matheny out of the minors when Phil was in Milwaukee and made him the Brewers' starting catcher. At the time I told Phil that Matheny's offensive projection was very weak. He knew, however, that Matheny was a super defensive catcher and a very intelligent player. If Matheny could just hit a little bit, and he was smart enough to do that, he could help the team. Well, the next manager to really go after and get Matheny was Cardinals manager Tony La Russa. Matheny is still not much of a hitter, but when both Phil Garner and Tony La Russa go out of their way to make you their starting catcher, you have to be a valuable ballplayer.

*Research by *Baseball Prospectus* writer Keith Woolner has shown that catchers by and large have no significant effect on pitchers' ERA. Given this new research, there appears to be no justifiable reason for a team to start a catcher, such as Mike Matheny or Brad Ausmus, solely because they do a good job "handling" pitchers. However, several of the Astros' starting pitchers have insisted that the Astros keep Brad Ausmus. The bottom line here is that when a team has a pitcher who is pitching as well as Roger Clemens has pitched for the Astros, and Clemens says that Brad Ausmus is playing a key part in Clemens' success, the Astros are going to keep Brad Ausmus.

# The Phil Garner Game Plan

**8/8/04:** Here are a few of the items Phil had in his game plan for the Astros:

(1) Increase the Astros' confidence level. For some reason, this team lacked confidence. A bad game, like yesterday's with four baserunning mistakes, shouldn't throw a team into a week-long funk. Phil preached (speaking of preaching, Phil's father and grandfather were both Baptist preachers) to these guys that this was a good team and they needed to adopt the attitude that they were winners and approach every game as though it was theirs to win. This is another reason why I think moving Bagwell up in the order was key. Bagwell was an experienced veteran. He needed to move up in the order where he could take a key role in the offense. From August 1 through the end of the season, Bagwell would lead the Astros in both Game Winning Runs Scored and Game Winning RBI.

(2) Improve the Astros' mental approach to hitting by taking every pitch of every at-bat seriously. Eliminate the three-pitch strikeout at-bats. Raise the pitch count for their opponents and make them get into their bullpen early and often in each series. Sooner or later the Astros would wear down their opponents and good things would start to happen.

(3) Clearly define everyone's role. Players may not always agree with what their role is, but each player on one of Phil Garner's teams always knows his role. Phil has confidence in his decisions, and therefore, so does his team.

(4) Use bench players to keep starting hitters fresh. Phil keeps a calendar of starts for his bench players and days off for his starting hitters. He makes sure that every starting hitter gets a rest every so often (although Berkman did start every game under Garner) and every bench player receives a start every so often.

(5) Be aggressive. Pitchers need to throw strikes and throw inside. Baserunners need to take bases when given the opportunity. Phil wanted his club to send a message to their opponents that the Astros were coming right at them.

Phil was slowly making inroads towards improving the psyche of this team and this, combined with a little tweaking in personnel and personnel usage, would some day very soon trigger an explosion of wins by this ball club. At least, that's what we kept telling ourselves.

**8/28/05:** Perhaps because they were tired of giving up home runs, Cubs pitchers pitched the Astros a bit more carefully this game and the result was eight Astros walks. Five of the walked Astros came around to score. This game was a good example of the work Phil Garner and batting coach Gary Gaetti were doing with the Astros' hitters, making them more selective, more patient, and just tougher outs in general.

Dan Miceli was placed on the disabled list and Russ Springer was purchased from the Astros' AAA farm club. Phil was pitching David Weathers in the seventh and Miceli in the eighth as his setup men. With Miceli on the DL and Weathers now in long relief, Phil Garner went with Springer in the seventh and Qualls in the eighth. Prior to today, Springer and Qualls only had one hold this year between them. Here it was, arguably the Astros' biggest game of the season thus far, and Phil had the guts to go with two new setup men. Springer got through the seventh, but Qualls gave up a run in the eighth and required help from Brad Lidge. Thanks to the help from Lidge, Springer and Qualls earned their first and second hold respectively this season.

**8/29/04:** Palmeiro had a big day for the Astros' today. Palmeiro got the start and Biggio got the day off because of the pitching matchup. As discussed previously, it is important to have bench players who have strengths where their starters have weaknesses, which enables a manager to use days off to improve his club. The Astros had that situation this season at every position with the exception of catcher.

**8/31/04:** I discussed earlier how Phil Garner was working on the Astros to make every pitch in every at-bat count. Well, this game was a perfect example of exactly that. The Reds' starting pitcher, Aaron Harang, had great stuff on this day. But the Astros kept battling—fouling off pitches, going deep into the count and raising Harang's pitch count. Harang was getting the Astros out, but the Astros were wearing him down. Eventually, fatigue set in and Harang surrendered back-to-back-to-back home runs to the Killer B's—Beltran, Bagwell and Berkman.

**9/16/04:** In the seventh inning, Qualls gave up three straight hits to lead off the inning and Phil left him in there. Qualls responded by retiring the next three Cardinals in order. It has to give a young pitcher confidence when a manager shows confidence in him during the heat of a pennant race. Qualls stated after the game, "[After I gave up three straight hits] I looked down at the bullpen and saw that no one was warming up. So, I thought I better start getting somebody out." This of course is vintage Phil Garner. He has a very good track record as far as developing young players. I would be remiss if I didn't also give pitching coach Jim Hickey credit for the development of the Astros' young pitchers. Most notably, Chad Qualls and Brandon Backe both pitched exceptionally well during the heat of the pennant race.

# Weathers Report

**8/12/04:** David Weathers took the loss in this one. Weathers had two losses and one blown save in the past week. After the blown save, Weathers responded to a reporter's question about the loss something to the effect of: "Things like that are going to happen at this point in the season when you have pitched as much as I have pitched." I interpreted Weathers' statement to mean one of two things: (1) bad things sometimes happen and it isn't really my fault; or (2) I have been overused and bad things happen if a pitcher is overused, so it really isn't my fault. Maybe I am being picky here, but either way, I take issue with Weathers' statement. I'd much rather hear a pitcher say to the press that he made a mistake and/or he let the team down.

Phil Garner doesn't mind if you disagree with him. In fact, he doesn't want to be surrounded by "yes men." He wants to hear your opinion and, if you disagree with him, he wants to hear your logic behind your opinion. At the same time, he doesn't criticize his players in the press and he expects the same in return. I figured that if Phil interpreted Weathers' statement to mean "I've been overused by my manager," Weathers would be gone as soon as Phil had control over his roster. Backstabbing to the press is something a manager cannot tolerate if he wants the respect of his players. Phil Garner once sent a young Gary Sheffield packing because he took a jab at Brewers management. He certainly wouldn't put up with it out of an old relief pitcher.

I may be way off base on this Weathers situation, but these were my thoughts at the time Weathers made his comments. I never did talk to Phil about Weathers, but I did notice that over the next two weeks Phil went out of his way to state to the press on more than one occasion that his bullpen was well rested.

**8/29/04:** The Astros acquired pitcher Dan Wheeler from the Mets and released pitcher David Weathers. Weathers wasn't a bad relief pitcher. He ranked third among Astros relievers in terms of "True Performance ERA," trailing only Lidge and Miceli. The two pitchers (Springer and Wheeler) the Astros picked up in the last couple of days both had good walk/strikeout ratios. To me, the release of Weathers and the acquisitions of pitchers with good walk/strikeout ratios were signs that Phil Garner now had control over the Astros and that this was a very good thing.

David Weathers was picked-up by the Florida Marlins and started a September game for the Marlins against the Cubs. He beat the Cubs in that key game, helping the Astros catch the Cubs. OK, David. All is forgiven.

# Bullpen Use

**8/13/04:** Astros closer Brad Lidge was brought into this game in the tenth inning with the score tied and pitched two shutout innings.

Phil Garner had a great closer this season in Brad Lidge and was using him in a manner in which he could perhaps steal an extra win or two. Phil would pitch Lidge with the score tied and on other occasions he would pitch him in the eighth. Most managers just save their closer for the ninth when they have a lead.

Below are the highlights from an e-mail I sent Phil on August 12 which includes findings and conclusions from a study conducted by Bill James on the most efficient use of a closer.

1. 100 runs saved by relief pitchers will have 70% more impact on the team's won-loss record than 100 runs saved by starting pitchers.

2. There are really two situations in which a run saved has a very high impact: When the game is tied and when you are one run ahead.

3. Each run saved in a tie game has more than eight times the impact of a run saved with a three-run lead.

4. The two situations in which the use of a relief ace is particularly helpful are when the teams are tied and when the team is ahead by one run. Statistically, no other situation is even remotely the same.

5. Modern relievers are very often used in situations (such as a three-run lead in the ninth) in which their presence in the game may be psychologically comforting, but has little practical benefit. The average team would win 97% of games with a three-run lead in the ninth even if it brought in a bad pitcher. Even bad pitchers don't often give up three runs in one inning.

6. The best situations in which to use a relief ace are:
   * two innings a game when the game is tied
   * two innings a game when you have a one-run lead
   * one inning at a time in other games when the game is close at the end and the relief ace hasn't been used for a day or two

These situations would create a workload of about 68 games and 113 innings per season.

7. Many modern relievers now are working 70 to 85 innings a season and they're not even working the right 75 innings.

8. "Saves" are one statistic that is overvalued at contract time. The result is that relievers are demanding to be in during a save situation. Consequently, for many of the current major league managers, this ego-driven or salary-driven use of statistics has taken precedence over the logical use of statistics.

9. A relief ace used in this suggested way wouldn't save 50 games, but he could win 20.

# Statistically, What Turned the Astros Around?

**8/15/04:** This was the game that started the Astros' 36-10 run to a wild card spot. Statistically speaking, there were two key changes that turned the Astros' season around: (1) The Astros increased their runs per game. Through July 31, the Astros scored 4.65 runs per game. After July 31, the Astros averaged 5.5 runs per game. (2) The Astros improved their win/loss record versus their Pythagorean win/loss record by six wins.

(1) The Increase in Runs:

(A) The batting order changes made the Astros' offense more efficient and put Jeff Bagwell and Carlos Beltran in positions where they could be more successful. Statistically, the benefits of the batting order change can be seen by comparing the Astros' actual runs to their Runs Created as determined by using Bill James' Runs Created Formula. Runs Created are the number of runs a team is expected to score given their "raw" offensive statistics. At the All-Star break, the Astros had scored 396 runs. James' Runs Created Formula indicated that the Astros should have scored 419 runs. Thus, we can conclude that the Astros lost 25 runs due to an inefficient batting order. Conversely, during September, the only full month the batting order changes were in effect, the Astros scored 140 runs, seven more than the 133 expected runs based on the Runs Created Formula. Conclusion: The Astros went from a batting order which cost them six or seven runs per month, to a batting order that gained them seven runs per month. That's a gain of 13 or 14 runs per month, or a run almost every other game. That's a huge improvement.

(B) Phil Garner changed the Astros' approach to hitting. Phil convinced the Astros to make every pitch while at bat mean something. The Astros went deep into counts, raising the pitch counts and wearing down opponents. The results were .2 more walks per game by Astro hitters and a lot more pitches thrown overall by opponents.

(C) While I cannot statistically prove it, there was a definite improvement in the team confidence level. Wins such as the comeback win on this date certainly helped the Astros believe that good things could happen to this club.

(D) An argument could be made that the acquisition of Beltran also increased the Astros' scoring. However, it should be noted that the Astros' scoring spike didn't occur when Beltran was acquired. It occurred when the batting order was changed.

(2) Pythagorean Wins,

A team's wins can be estimated by the Pythagorean Formula, which is a (team's runs)$^2$ / (runs scored$^2$ + runs allowed$^2$). The one player who can cause the largest difference between a team's actual wins and its Pythagorean wins is a team's closer.

At the end of July, the Astros had 52 wins. The Pythagorean Formula indicated that they should have had 57 wins. Thus, the Astros were -5 in Pythagorean wins. In other words, the Astros had lost five more games than they should have given the number of runs the Astros scored and allowed. By the end of the season the Astros were +1 in Pythagorean wins, having won 92 games. The Pythagorean Formula indicated that they should have won 91 games. The Astros picked up six Pythagorean Wins over the last 58 games. There were two main reasons why the Astros were able to do this: Lidge was simply great, and Phil used Lidge in the most efficient manner.

Now, yes, I realize that there are other factors that could have contributed to the six extra wins, such as clutch hitting. However, an increase of six Pythagorean wins in just 58 games is a huge difference. In order to get those six extra wins, both the Astros' bullpen and the use thereof had to be major factors. Lidge had to be great (which he was) and Phil had to use Lidge in the most efficient manner possible (which he did).

## And Phil's Opinion

I asked Phil Garner a couple months after the season ended what was the reason for the great turnaround and Phil gave all the credit to his players, saying that they stepped up, played great and simply refused to lose. And no doubt, they did. It was simply beautiful watching these guys play baseball over the last 46 games. It wasn't just one or two guys playing well. They all played well. Even our much maligned catchers, Brad Ausmus and Raul Chavez, played well. A team can't go 36-10 without everyone contributing. The Astros players were simply great these last 46 games.

# Double Switching

**8/17/04:** In response to criticism in the *Houston Chronicle*, the following are highlights from an e-mail I sent to Phil Garner on double switching.

**When Ahead:** Defense is the key. Only double switch when it improves your defense. There is no strong need not to have your pitcher bat. I assume the double switches you have been making with Biggio are to improve the defense.

**When Behind:** Offense is the key. Only double switch when it improves the offense. There are quite a few managers in baseball who will screw this one up and pull a double switch only to have a weak hitting infielder leading off the next inning instead of a good hitting pinch-hitter.

**When Tied:** The pitcher is the key. This is the situation where the most double switches occur because when the score is tied, a manager wants to keep his best pitcher in the game but also the manager would want to pinch-hit for the pitcher when he comes to bat.

**Two Don'ts:** (1) Don't double switch your big four out of the game—Beltran, Bagwell, Berkman and Kent. (2) Don't double switch early in a game.

Phil responded to my e-mail on double switching with an e-mail of his own that included the following comments:

(1) Your analysis is good. I agree with most of your assessments.

(2) I do double switch with Biggio to get a better defensive player into the game.

(3) I also switch to get my best hitter off the bench (Lamb) two at-bats in a game when we are down.

(4) The moron [writer] did not understand that I took Berkman and Baggy out because we had a big lead and I wanted the bench players to play and get the AB's.

(5) Find some catching!

# Study on Managers

In 2003, I did a study in an effort to evaluate major league managers. In the study, each manager earned a "win" each time he took over a club which improved in his first season as manager. Conversely, a manager earned a "loss" each time he took over a club whose record declined in his first season as manager. Each manager also earned a "win" each time his team had a worse record in their first season without him. Conversely, a "loss" was earned each time a team improved in their first season without him. The result was that there were five current managers (as of 2003) who were +3 ("wins" minus "losses"). Bobby Cox (4-1), Lou Pinella (4-1), Frank Robinson (5-2), Joe Torre (5-2), and Tony La Russa (4-1). There were only two "-3" or worse managers working in the majors in 2003: Bob Boone (0-3) and Jimmy Williams (0-5). The best record at that time for unemployed managers belonged to Jack McKeon (6-2) and Phil Garner (4-0). McKeon was hired by the Marlins later in the 2003 season and the Marlins won a World Championship. Garner was hired in 2004 to replace Williams (0-5) and the Astros made it within one game of the World Series.

# Steve Stone and the Cubs

**8/26/04:** The Astros really needed to take three out of the four games in this series with the Cubs. After this day's loss the Astros' backs were against the wall. They could not afford to lose another game to the Cubs and expect to catch them for the wild card. In fact, Cubs announcer Steve Stone stated after the game that if the Cubs could win just one of these last three games with the Astros, they could forget about the Astros for this season.

**8/27/04:** The Astros came out of the gate with four runs in the first and stomped the Cubs 15-7. Cubs announcer Steve Stone stated after the game that if the Cubs could win just one of the next two games with the Astros, the Astros' season would be over.

**8/28/04:** The Astros scored five runs in the first two innings and hung on to beat the Cubs 7-6. Cubs announcer Steve Stone stated after the game that if the Cubs could win just the next game with the Astros, the Astros' season would be over.

**8/29/04:** Once again with the Astros' backs against the wall, the Astros scored early on their way to a 10-3 blow out. After the game, Cubs announcer Steve Stone stated that the Cubs' failure to knock the Astros out of the wild card race this weekend may come back to haunt them. When the Cubs failed to win the wild card, manager Dusty Baker and several players chastised announcer Steve Stone for making negative comments about the Cubs. Stone was fired as the Cubs' announcer after the season. I heard someone say (I think it was Mike on the "Mike and Mike in the Morning Show") that "Anytime you look to the broadcast booth for [the cause of] your problems, you are looking in the wrong direction."

Why did the Cubs lose? Well, I don't think the Cubs lost it as much as the Astros just took control of the wild card race, winning 36 of their last 46 games. However, one problem that the Cubs had was the fact that their lineup had too many similar hitters. Their lineup was full of high slugging percentage players who had low on-base percentages. This lack of good on-base percentage hitters resulted in the Cubs hitting a lot of solo home runs instead of getting three-run homers. Moreover, if the ball didn't go out of the park, the Cubs lost. The poster boy for the Cubs' lineup was Sammy Sosa, who has been criticized for setting a record for the least RBI of any player hitting 35 home runs or more. RBI are a function of three things: a player's slugging percentage, the number of at-bats a player receives, and the on-base percentage of the players in front of him. In fact,

I once devised a formula to roughly estimate a player's RBI total for the season. The formula was to multiply a hitter's at-bats times his slugging percentage times his team's on-base percentage. Let's test the formula on the Cubs' four big RBI men:

| | ABs | Slug % | Team OB% | Expected RBI | Actual RBI | Difference |
|---|---|---|---|---|---|---|
| Alou | 601 | .557 | .328 | 110 | 106 | -4 |
| Lee | 605 | .504 | .328 | 100 | 98 | -2 |
| Ramirez | 546 | .578 | .328 | 104 | 103 | -1 |
| Sosa | 478 | .517 | .328 | 81 | 80 | -1 |

This chart indicates that Sosa's RBI total was as expected for a player given his slugging percentage, number of at-bats and team on-base percentage. Thus, I contend that Sosa's lack of RBI are not all his fault, but much of the blame should be placed on Cubs management for the lack of good on-base percentage hitters in the lineup. By the way, in the Cubs' last three victories over the Astros in 2004, all three game-winning RBI were by Sammy Sosa.

# Ensberg vs. Lamb

**8/28/04:** Morgan Ensberg went on the DL. Mike Lamb started for the next 21 games at third base. Lamb simply did a great job for the Astros and Lamb was a big part of the reason the Astros would go on and win the wild card. For the season, Lamb out hit Ensberg, but Ensberg had the edge defensively.

**9/27/04:** Ensberg was now healthy and also hitting the ball well. Phil had a decision to make. In Milwaukee, every decision we had to make was based on what was best for the Brewers in the long run. Thus, we both had the philosophy of pick your best and write him in the lineup every day. However, this was a pennant race, short term decisions for individual games now out weighed any long term plan. I recommended that Phil take a game-by-game approach and start the best third base choice for that given game. Phil, however, was confident that if he just stayed the course, the Astros were going to prevail. So Mike Lamb went back to the bench and Morgan Ensberg resumed full-time starting third base duties. Lamb did make one situational start. That start came against Matt Morris in game six of the NLCS.

**10/20/04:** Mike Lamb made his first start in the postseason. For game six, with Ensberg struggling a bit and given that Lamb had hit three home runs off Morris this season, Phil opted to go with Lamb. Lamb responded with his fourth home run of the season off Morris.

# Joseph's Day

**9/1/04:** With the Astros in Cincinnati to play the Reds, I decided to drive down to the game, which is about 90 miles away from our home in Lynn, Indiana. I hadn't seen Phil in a few years. The last couple of times he was in Cincinnati with the Tigers and Brewers I didn't make it down to see him. I probably wouldn't have gone down to the game this season if not for my youngest son Joseph, who really wanted to go down and see his favorite player, Jeff Bagwell, play. I had my father, who lives in Cincinnati, meet us at the game so he could watch Joseph while I was down in the clubhouse meeting with Phil. However, Phil was good enough to invite us all down to the clubhouse.

Phil and I went over a few things, focusing on his September call-ups and the wild card race. It appeared that he would get everyone up he wanted except Willy Taveras, who Phil wanted to use as a pinch-runner. The resistance from management stemmed from the fact that teams generally hate to start the clock on major league service time that affects arbitration and free agent starting dates. If Taveras could net the Astros one extra win, however, it could be huge. I suggested that Phil push hard for Taveras, and a few days later he was added to the roster. As for the wild card race, I told Phil that the Astros had the second best runs scored to runs allowed ratio of all the wild card hopefuls, second only to the Cubs. He felt very confident, however, that if the Astros could get close enough to put themselves in the Cubs' rearview mirror, we would win it.

We covered a few more things. Phil talked to Joseph about basketball and my father and Phil spent some time talking about baseball right up until game time. My father has often told me what a big thrill it was for him as a young boy to spend a day at a Cleveland Indians game with Hall of Famer Tris Speaker. I suspect Joseph will one day tell the story of what a thrill it was to sit in the Astros' clubhouse and talk about baseball and basketball with Phil Garner.

Our seats were in the first row, right behind the Astros' dugout. After Austin Kearns of the Reds struck out to end the first inning, Raul Chavez, who was catching, came back and rolled the baseball across the top of the dugout to Joseph. If you recall, one of my three original recommendations for Phil Garner on August 1, 2004, was to replace Chavez. Anyway, when Joseph first got the ball, he had this big smile on his face. Then it quickly faded as he turned towards me, looked real serious, and said, "That's not the guy you're trying to get rid of, is it?"

Later in the game, I was talking with two relatives of Astros pitcher Chad

Harville. They told me that Chad had taken a couple of losses he had with the Astros real hard and that he was a little concerned about his spot on the roster. I told them I had just talked to Phil Garner earlier in the day and Phil had a lot of good things to say about Chad (which was true). I told them to tell Chad not to worry about anything, to just go out and pitch. Harville went on a hot streak for about the next three weeks without giving up a run. I doubt that my comments had anything to do with Harville's streak, but the reason I included this last story is because sometimes we forget that ballplayers are no different from us. They have fathers who drive to games to see them play and they have self doubts when things aren't going well.

When the game was over and the Astros left the field and headed into the dugout, Phil Garner looked up and said to my son, "Good luck with basketball, Joseph." Joseph's day, which was already a great one, was just made even better.

# Pitching Decisions

**9/3/04:** Phil Garner uses a straight five-man rotation. However, with the Astros hot and the shot at the wild card spot becoming a real possibility, I sent Phil a recommended rotation on September 2 that had Oswalt and Clemens pitching on four days rest the rest of the season with the other three starting pitchers filling in as needed. This recommended rotation would enable Oswalt to get one extra start before the playoffs. One extra start for Oswalt in a close race could be huge. The problem was Oswalt was nursing a rib injury and Clemens was nursing a leg injury. Both could use an extra day or so. Thus, Phil withheld changing the rotation until September 16, when Phil moved up Oswalt and Backe ahead of Pete Munro. By moving Oswalt and Backe ahead of Munro, Phil was able to get an extra start out of both of them, taking away starts from Munro and Hernandez. In their extra starts in the last two games of the season, both Oswalt and Backe picked up wins.

Here is the expected games started for the Astros' pitchers beginning 9/3 if using a straight five-man rotation:

Clemens-6; Hernandez-6; Munro-6; Oswalt-5; Backe-5; Redding-1

The Actual Starts:

Clemens-6; Oswalt-6; Backe-6; Hernandez-5; Munro-5; Redding-1

Again, one extra start for Oswalt and Backe, one less start for Hernandez and Munro.

**9/4/04:** Approximately once a week I sent Phil Garner the Astros pitchers' True Performance ERA. The interesting thing was that reliever Russ Springer at this time had a great traditional ERA. However, his True Performance ERA was below average. The game previous to this one was a perfect example as to why. In the September 3 game, Springer came on in the seventh to relieve Clemens with two on and two outs. Jack Wilson greeted Springer with a triple to drive in two runs, runs that would be charged to Clemens. Springer then walked the next batter before getting the third out. Thus, Springer's pitching line would be three batters faced, a triple, walk and an out. No runs. Under traditional ERA formula, Springer's ERA would improve (decrease) after this outing. Conversely, his True Performance ERA would decline (increase).

Well, because Springer had a good traditional ERA and a better radar gun rating, Springer stayed ahead of Wheeler in the Astros' bullpen. In the old days with Milwaukee, I would have been fighting to get Phil to move Wheeler ahead of Springer in the Astros' bullpen. However, Phil had the Astros rolling so I merely sent the True Performance ERA faxes showing that in terms of True Performance ERA, Wheeler was better. In retrospect, maybe I should have fought for Wheeler because Springer lost game four for the Astros in the Division Series against the Braves, a game in which Wheeler did not pitch. Here are the postseason stats for Springer and Wheeler:

| | G | IP | H | R | ER | BB | SO | Record |
|---|---|---|---|---|---|---|---|---|
| Dan Wheeler | 5 | 8 | 4 | 0 | 0 | 0 | 9 | 1-win, 0-losses |
| Russ Springer | 2 | 2 | 3 | 4 | 4 | 1 | 5 | 0-wins, 1-loss |

# Stat Fact

**9/4/04:** Here are a couple of little-known statistical facts:

(1) For most major league hitters the percentage of flyballs hit do not increase when there is a man on third base. This means that almost all sacrifice flys are random occurrences and not something that a hitter can successfully try to do.

(2) Baseball games are not won by making outs. Games are won by getting hits and getting on base. Hitting behind runners and moving runners along are great concepts, but almost all games are won by the team with the "best net" (the team which puts the most runners on base and has the most total bases). In this game, the Astros had a better net than the Pirates. Having said that, the Astros also had three sacrifices in the game on September 4, which lead to three important runs. Berkman and Kent hit sacrifice flys in the first and Chavez had a sacrifice bunt in the sixth that lead to a run. So yes, the Astros out hit the Pirates in this game, but they also showed that they can do the little things which can, once in a while, steal a win.

# The Bullingers

**9/6/04:** Kirk Bullinger was lit up in the ninth. With Miceli due back soon from the DL, Bullinger's role on the staff was now in jeopardy.

**9/20/04:** As a result of Ausmus' concussion, the Astros had to purchase a catcher, Chris Tremie, from the minors. In order to make room for Tremie, the Astros released Bullinger. Three weeks earlier when I was in Cincinnati, as I watched the Astros' pitchers make the long walk from the bullpen to the dugout after the game, Bullinger had the look of a man that knew he had lost his role on the team. Maybe he just looked that way because I believed he had pitched himself off the roster. Moreover, in terms of "True Performance ERA," Bullinger was the Astros' worst reliever.

It is ironic how things work sometimes. In 1994, when I worked for the Cubs, I sat in on a coaches' meeting where the Cubs had to decide which one of their bullpen pitchers would make an emergency start, lefty Dave Otto or righty Jim Bullinger (big brother to Kirk Bullinger). During that coaches' meeting, I pointed out that Bullinger was equally tough on both lefties and righties, which is an indication Bullinger would be just as successful starting as he was relieving.

One difference between starting and relieving is that, as a relief pitcher, your manager has some control over who you face in a game. For example, a righty reliever who is tough on righties could be brought in to face three righty batters. However, who a starting pitcher faces in a game is dictated by the opposing manager who makes out the lineup card. Thus, that same righty reliever who is tough on righties, as a starter may see the opposing manager stack his lineup with lefties. Since Jim Bullinger was equally tough on righties and lefties, in a starting situation the opposing lineup wouldn't matter. We voted, and Bullinger got the start. Bullinger pitched well and stayed in the rotation. Thus, I may have had a hand in the promotion of one Bullinger and the demotion of another.

# Barry Bonds

**8/20/04:** I e-mailed Phil concerning my recommendation on when to walk Barry Bonds. If you took the statistical quiz earlier in this book, you know that an intentionally walked batter has a better chance of scoring a run than the next batter has a chance of hitting into a double play. In general, an intentional walk is what is called a "one run" strategy, which can result in a big inning for your opponent. Thus, for that reason, intentional walks are usually only recommended late in a game and usually with two outs. However, Barry Bonds is a whole different story. Thus, I sent Phil the following recommendation:

> Outs are the most important thing when it comes to Barry Bonds and intentional walks. Always walk Bonds with two outs. Never walk Bonds with no outs. With one out, let the baserunners and score dictate.

Here is what happened with Bonds in the series:

**With two outs and baserunners on**, Bonds batted seven times. Six times Bonds was intentionally walked. Bonds did NOT score after any of these intentional walks. The one time Phil did not walk Bonds was with two outs and a runner on in the first inning of the second game with Oswalt pitching. I didn't ask Phil, but my guess is that Oswalt insisted on pitching to Bonds. The result of Oswalt pitching to Bonds in that instance was an RBI triple for Bonds.

**With one out and runners on base**, Bonds had one at-bat. Well, sort of. He was hit by a pitch.

**With two outs and no one on base**, Bonds batted just twice. Phil pitched to Bonds both times. Once Bonds tripled and scored and once Bonds popped out.

**With one out and no one on base**, Bonds batted twice. Once Bonds made an out. Once Bonds walked and scored.

**With no outs**, Bonds batted just twice in the series. Phil pitched to him both times, and once Bonds popped out and once Bonds reached base on an error by Jeff Kent.

To summarize, in the series the Astros pitched to Bonds with no outs and/ or with no runners on base, hit Bonds with one out and runners on base, and intentionally walked Bonds with two outs and runners on base. Except for Oswalt pitching to Bonds in the first inning of game two, Bonds did not factor in any of the Giants' runs in their two victories over the Astros.

# The Internet and the Radio

I spent most of the 2004 season watching the Astros' games written out pitch by pitch on the Internet. During most of the games this season, my boys would grab me away from the computer to go outside and play baseball or basketball. However, this series in San Francisco started late and my boys were in bed so I was able to watch the games on the computer uninterrupted. In retrospect, I wished the boys had interrupted me because the games were so painful, frustrating and stressful to watch on the computer. By the start of the seventh inning of the last game of the series, the Astros had only scored one run in their last 23 innings against the Giants. Then with the Astros down 3-0 and the end of their postseason hopes just nine outs away, the Astros began their climb back. In the seventh inning, Beltran walked, stole two bases, then scored on a single by Berkman. In the eighth, with one out, Vizcaino singled, and Ausmus singled. Ensberg then grounded into a force to score pinch-runner Bruntlett. As the Astros entered the ninth, they still trailed 3-2. The Astros were now just three outs away from the end of their season, but they came out in the ninth swinging. Beltran singled. Bagwell followed with an infield single. This brought Berkman to the plate. I stared at the computer, waiting for something to happen. Sometimes the person who was updating the game on the Internet would fall behind. Maybe he was taking a restroom break. Sometimes his breaks would happen in a key situation with a full count. I would sit there for more than 20 minutes waiting as my blood pressure rose waiting for something to happen. Then the guy would come back and post two innings at once. So there I am waiting, two on and no outs, not knowing if three Astros outs would post next or three Astros runs. Then it flashed up on the screen, "HOME RUN BERKMAN." I jumped out of my chair and shouted, "YES!" After that the Astros added two more runs and came away with a critical win.

The phrase "must-win" is over used. But, this really was a must-win for the Astros. If the Giants won this game and nothing else changed, the Giants would have beaten the Astros out by one game. As it was, the Astros had to go 8-1 the rest of the way to win the wild card.

Three quick stories from way back:

(1) My father tells me when he was a young Reds fan, the Reds didn't broadcast a lot of games on radio, but the radio station would give updates between half innings. The radio station would play songs until the

half inning was over. When the Reds were batting, my father used to root for extra songs to be played. This would mean that the Reds would have been batting for a long time and probably would have scored a few runs. Of course, when the Reds' opponents were batting, he would be rooting for just a couple songs to play. In between songs, there would also be that pause where he would either be rooting or not rooting for another song. My father said the worst thing was when the Reds would be up, there would be a long five-song inning, and he would be certain the Reds scored four or five runs but somehow they failed to score any.

(2) One time when the Reds were playing St. Louis, my grandfather was having friends over and they were listening to the Cincinnati station that gave the half inning updates between songs. My dad was able to pick up KMOX in St. Louis on his bedroom radio. They were carrying the game live. During a break in the action my dad walked into the room where everyone was waiting for the Cincinnati station to give a report and heard someone making a prediction about that inning, such as "I bet Musial will hit a home run this inning." Of course, my dad had just heard that inning so he said, "No, I bet Musial will strike out." After several more trips between the two rooms, everyone thought my dad was some sort of baseball genius.

(3) The next broadcasting innovation to follow the half inning update was the ticker tape. Play-by-play for road games would be sent via ticker tape. Ticker tape was so named because messages would be typed out on a continuous paper tape. While it was typing out on the tape, the sound it made was tick, tick, tick. Anyway, the Reds' announcer, former Yankees pitching star Waite Hoyt, would read the play-by-play as it came over the tape. Sometimes, however, the tape would break and Hoyt would have to stall until the tape was fixed by adding a fictitious trip to the mound or a few harmless foul balls that never really happened. Once, Hoyt said it took a very long time to fix the tape and by the time the tape was fixed, Hoyt had described to the listening audience 24 straight foul balls.

# Playoff Roster

**10/1/04:** I sent Phil a fax that contained two things before this game: the revised True Performance ERAs for the Astros' pitchers and my recommended playoff roster.

Now baseball people have varied opinions on how many pitchers a team should carry in the postseason. Most agree that it should be at least one less pitcher than what was carried on the roster during the regular season because there is one less starting pitcher needed in the postseason. I went through Phil's games since the rosters were expanded and counted the number of pitchers and non-pitchers Phil used in his games and came to the conclusion that, based on the way Phil managed the last month, eleven pitchers (or one less than Phil used during the season) was the number best suited to the Astros' needs, or at least to the Astros' needs that last month of the regular season. It was close, but the eleventh pitcher looked to be just a little more valuable than the fifteenth hitter. Two other factors that weighed in on the side of the eleventh pitcher included: the possibility of back-to-back extra inning games (like the Red Sox and Yankees ended up playing in the ALCS) would definitely make the eleventh pitcher more important than the fifteenth hitter; and Astro starter Brandon Backe was proving he was a decent hitter and would probably be OK as a pinch-hitter if it became necessary.

So here was the playoff roster I sent Phil, the same playoff roster used by the Astros:

Starting Hitters
Craig Biggio
Carlos Beltran
Jeff Bagwell
Lance Berkman
Jeff Kent
Morgan Ensberg
Jose Vizcaino
Brad Ausmus

Bench
Eric Bruntlett
Raul Chavez
Adam Everett

Mike Lamb
Jason Lane
Orlando Palmeiro

Starting Pitchers
Roy Oswalt
Roger Clemens
Brandon Backe
Pete Munro

Bullpen
Brad Lidge
Chad Qualls
Dan Wheeler
Dan Miceli
Mike Gallo
Russ Springer
Chad Harville

# Game #162, The Clincher

**10/3/04:** A win today would mean a wild card spot for the Astros. It would also mean that the Astros had gone 40-18 since the morning of August 1, the day I first called Phil Garner. Phil had planned on pitching Roger Clemens on three days rest, but Clemens was scratched because of the flu. In place of Clemens, Brandon Backe would start.

Bottom of the second, score 0-0: Kent grounds out; Ensberg walks; Vizcaino singles to right; Ensberg to third; Vizcaino steals second; Backe singles to right scoring Ensberg and Vizcaino. Astros lead 2-0.

Bottom of the third, Astros lead 2-0: Beltran flys to right; Bagwell safe on error; Bagwell steals second; Berkman doubles; Astros now lead 3-0; Berkman steals third; Kent singles to left; Astros now lead 4-0; Kent steals second; Ensberg grounds to second for the second out; Vizcaino singles home Kent. Astros up 5-0.

Now at this point I was certain we had done it. We had won 36 out of the last 46 games and caught five teams in the wild card race. Then the thought occurred to me that maybe I didn't do anything. I'm just sitting here on my couch. It was Phil Garner and hitting coach Gary Gaetti who changed the mental approach of the Astros' hitters. It was the Astros' players themselves who stepped it up and got it done. What had I done? Then TV announcer and former major league pitcher Rick Sutcliffe states, as if on cue, that he believed the turning point for this Astros team was the change in the batting order that moved Jeff Bagwell from sixth to the middle of the order. Yes, I thought, maybe I did do something. After all, it was my e-mail that caused Phil to move Bagwell up in the order. Since August 1, Bagwell had lead the Astros in both game winning runs (eight) and game winning RBI (eight). And there was that other recommendation I made on August 1, in the name of Brandon Backe, who just happened to be on the mound pitching the Astros to the wild card spot. So, maybe it was acceptable for me to use the word "we." Maybe.

The Rockies scored two runs in the sixth to cut the lead to 5-2. I knew that all we had to do was get Brad Lidge in and the game was over. Miceli gave up a double to Helton to lead off the eighth, Castilla and Burnitz both groundout moving Helton around to score. Closser singled with two outs bringing the tying run to the plate and Phil Garner to the mound. Phil brought Brad Lidge into the game. Lidge was a man possessed. K; K; K; K. The Astros win!

# Postseason Strategy

**10/10/04 Division Series Game 4:** The key question heading into game four was would Phil Garner start Roger Clemens on three days rest or would he go with Pete Munro. Phil had the Braves down two games to one. The Astros were at home. There was absolutely no doubt in my mind that Phil would go for, and he did, the knock out punch with the big guy, the Rocket, Roger Clemens.

This was a game the Astros should have won. Things just didn't go the Astros' way:

1. The Astros had a better net than the Braves, yet lost. It was the Astros' only postseason game this year where the team with the better net didn't win. Again, net is times on base + total bases + sacrifices and stolen bases - outs used.

2. John Smoltz gave up four hits in the final two innings, yet the Astros didn't score.

3. The winning run off Springer in the top of the ninth was hard to swallow. Springer struck out the first two batters, then hit Rafael Furcal. J. D. Drew was now at the plate. Drew had struck out the last two times to the plate. For the series, Drew was 2-for-15 with both hits being infield singles. Yet Drew hit his first out of the infield hit in the series and the Braves scored.

4. Even when things went right for the Astros they went wrong. Jason Lane got a two-out single for the Astros in the eighth which forced Phil Garner to pinch-hit for Brad Lidge. Thus, Springer came on and pitched the ninth instead of Lidge.

**Double Switches:** On August 16, I sent an e-mail to Phil Garner in regard to double switches. In that fax, I made two statements that conflicted in this game: (1) When the score is tied, the pitcher is the key. This is the situation where most double switches should occur. A manager wants to both keep his best pitcher in the game but also have a batter come to bat when the pitcher is due; and; (2) Do not double switch with your best players. In the Astros' case that would be Beltran, Bagwell, Berkman and Kent.

With Kent making the last out in the seventh, and Lidge entering the game in the eighth, this put these two statements on double switching in conflict. The pitcher's spot would be up fifth in the bottom of the eighth for the Astros with Beltran, Bagwell, Berkman and Kent to follow. Phil either had to double switch Kent out of the game for a much lesser hitter in Bruntlett, or risk the fifth spot coming to bat in the eighth. Well, with Smoltz coming in to pitch in the eighth, and the six, seven, eight and nine batters due up in Ensberg, Vizcaino, Ausmus and Lane, three of which were righthanded batters, the odds were that the fifth spot in the order would not come to bat. Thus, Phil could leave Kent in the game. Lidge could pitch the rest of the eighth and then the ninth and Phil would have the heart of the order intact for the bottom of the ninth and an Astros win. Phil decided to play these odds. Smoltz retired the first two Astros in the eighth, so it looked like the gamble would pay off. Then with two outs, Ausmus and Lane got back-to-back hits off Smoltz. Phil was then forced to pinch-hit for Lidge. Still, it looked like no harm no foul when Springer struck out the first two batters in the ninth. Then the Braves scored a run on a hit batter, a stolen base, and Drew's first hit out of the infield of the series. Two bad breaks, right? The Astros, however, still had their big four intact in the bottom of the ninth. Now they just needed to score two runs instead of one to win. Beltran struck out, but then Bagwell and Berkman got back-to-back hits. This brought up Jeff Kent, Mr. RBI, and my thought was that sooner or later the luck in this game had to change. Kent is going to hit a double and game over, the Astros win. Kent hit a double of sorts— a double play and the game was over. After the game, Phil was criticized for both his decision not to walk Drew and not to double switch Kent out of the game. In my opinion, Phil made the right decision in both cases, it just didn't work out.

Two other comments: (1) A case could be made that this was the game that cost the Astros a trip to the World Series. If the Astros had won this game, Oswalt would have had two starts against the Cardinals instead of just one and that one extra start by Oswalt could have been all the Astros needed to beat the Cardinals. (2) After this game, Springer did not appear in the Astros' last eight postseason games.

**10/11/04 Game 5 Division Series:** The Astros won their first ever postseason series. Just for trivia's sake, the final out of the game: Dan Wheeler pitching to Chipper Jones, flyball to left field where Jason Lane makes the catch. Dan Wheeler had pitched a perfect ninth inning to end the game. It was Wheeler's first appearance for the Astros in the postseason, but it was a very important inning for the Astros because Wheeler's perfect inning earned him key innings in the upcoming NLCS, innings which would help keep the Astros alive in that series.

**10/14/04 NLCS Game 2:** Back on August 12, I sent Phil an e-mail on a study on bullpen use. Most managers will only use their closer when they are ahead in the ninth. However, the study showed that managers should use a closer for two innings (not just the ninth) and whenever tied or ahead (not just ahead). Phil told me at the time that he was using and he would continue to use his closer Lidge as the study dictated with two slight variations: (1) Phil would use his closer as early as the seventh inning to get out of a seventh inning jam when ahead, and (2) Phil had a problem with using Lidge in the eighth inning of a tied road game. Phil told me that it was his experience that using your closer on the road in the eighth inning of a tied game rarely ever worked out. What always seemed to happen was that you both lost the game and wore out your closer.

Well, in the eighth inning of this game with the score tied on the road, Phil had the choice between Miceli and his closer Lidge. Phil stuck by the strategy he used all season and brought in Miceli. Unfortunately, Miceli got lit up like a roman candle.

**10/17/04 NLCS Game 5:** Cardinal Manager Tony La Russa was faced with the same situation as Phil Garner faced in Game 2. Unlike Garner, La Russa brought in his closer, Isringhausen. La Russa's strategy didn't work either, as Isringhausen lost the game in the ninth. The longer Phil manages in the majors, the harder it gets to win an argument with him. One of the reasons I enjoy working for Phil Garner is he is so statistically sound. Phil probably managed his closer more closely to the findings on the study on efficient bullpen use than any manager in baseball. And, as a result, statistics indicate that as many as six "extra" wins could be attributed to Phil Garner's use of the Astros' closer in the Astros' last 58 games.

**10/18/04 NLCS Game 6:** The big decision heading in to Game 6 was who the Astros were going to start. The Astros could pitch Clemens on three days rest and then Oswalt in Game 7, or they could pitch Munro in Game 6 and have a well rested Clemens for Game 7. Munro or Clemens, that was the big decision heading into Game 6.

I called Phil the next day, an off day for the series, and the conversation went something like this:

**Doug Decatur:** I thought I would weigh in on the Clemens/Munro decision.

**Phil Garner:** Good, I'd like to hear what you have to say.

**DD:** If Clemens wants the ball, it has to be Clemens…as long as Oswalt is OK.

**PG:** Well, that's the problem. Roger would do whatever we ask, but Roy [Oswalt] can't go again on just three days rest. He's running on empty.

**DD:** I was worried about that, no strikeouts in his last outing when pitching on five days rest.

**PG:** Yes, I just can't send Roy back out there for more than a couple innings the rest of this series.

**DD:** So, Munro in Game 6.

**PG:** Yes, Munro in Game 6, then Clemens will pitch our next game whenever that is.

**DD:** One more thing, I have a birthday in two days. How about an Astros win on my birthday.

**PG:** Well, I'd like to give you that birthday present a day early. [Game 7 fell on my birthday, but Game 6 was the day before.]

**DD:** Yeah, that would be great. I'll take the win a day early.

One of the things that makes Phil a good manager is that he protects his players. In the paper the next day, Phil stated that he made his decision to start Munro because he wanted to give Clemens four days rest. Phil never mentioned that Oswalt was the reason for the decision. If he had, the press might have ripped Oswalt. Ironically, with the discussion focused on Munro and Clemens for starting Game 6, the decision was based on neither of them.

One year later, a "healthy" Roy Oswalt would win the NLCS MVP Award by winning two games against the Cardinals and sending the Astros to their first ever World Series.

# Astros Owner Drayton McLane

Three stories about about Astros owner Drayton McLane:

(1) The Astros finished the season with 33 players on their active roster. For the postseason, the Astros had to pare their roster down to 25. The eight Astros players who didn't make the 25-man postseason roster could have been sent home for the winter. Such a move would have saved the Astros money. However, owner Drayton McLane kept the eight players with the ballclub. In fact, McLane went to the extra expense of taking the players on the road in the playoffs to both Atlanta and St. Louis. Why? Loyalty. To McLane these eight players helped the Astros win the wild card and, therefore, they deserved to be there for the playoffs. If it cost the Astros money, so be it.

As a side note, during the 2005 playoffs, Phil Garner stated that one reason for the success of rookies Chris Burke and Willy Taveras in the 2005 postseason was the fact that both were with the team the season before and had been able to experience the postseason, even if they weren't on the 25-man active roster.

(2) When Drayton McLane hired Phil Garner as Interim Manager, McLane promised Phil that he would be given a chance to win with the Astros this season. On August 14, the Astros were four games under .500. Many believed that the Astros should throw in the towel for the season and trade free agent to be Jeff Kent. However, McLane said no. He had promised Phil Garner that the Astros were going to try to win this season, and he was going to stand by his promise.

(3) McLane hired Garner as the Astros' Interim Manager because McLane knew Garner from his church. McLane knew that Phil was first and foremost a good person, and to Drayton McLane that was the most important quality of a winner.

In conclusion, in today's jaded business world of sports, Astros owner Drayton McLane is a breath of fresh air. McLane is a man who believes loyalty, honesty and integrity are the building blocks of a winning organization.

# The End of a Good Run, October 21, NLCS Game 7

After six games, both the Astros and the Cardinals had the exact same batting average (.246), runs scored (29), and ERA (4.80). For the sixth game in the series, the visiting team scored in the top of the first. And, for the seventh game in a row, the visiting team lost.

October 21 is my birthday. With the Astros playing on my birthday, it reminded me of my youth when the Reds played three times on my birthday in the 1970s. In 1972, the Reds beat Sal Bando's Oakland A's in Game 6 of the World Series. In 1975, the Reds lost to the Red Sox in Game 6 of the World Series. (This game was considered to be one of the greatest games in baseball history.) In 1976 the Reds won their second straight World Series by beating the Yankees in Game 4.

Anyway, this was going to be a good birthday. My oldest son Stephen shares the same birthday as mine. My parents drove up from Cincinnati to help Stephen and I celebrate his 13th birthday and my 46th. After an early dinner, we all took off for my youngest son Joseph's first basketball scrimmage of the season. We returned home just in time for the Astros game to start.

I was feeling good about this game until the sixth inning. In the sixth, the Cardinals chased Clemens out of the game, my parents back to Cincinnati, and my wife and kids to bed. I was left alone to watch the last nine painful Astros outs.

The last seven Astros would go down in order. First the killer B's, Biggio, Beltran, Bagwell and Berkman. In the ninth, Kent, Ensberg and finally Vizcaino on a groundout to second base. End of ballgame. End of season.

In the locker room in St. Louis, Phil Garner looked at the faces of his players and reflected on the season. Phil would tell his players that he loved them and just how proud he was of them, their 36-10 run, their first postseason series win in Astros history, and their epic battle with the Cardinals.

Meanwhile, in my living room in Lynn, Indiana, I looked at my now blank TV screen and my half-eaten piece of birthday cake and reflected on the day's events. No, I didn't get an Astros win for a birthday present. But, there was Stephen's 13th birthday and Joseph's basketball game. I brushed my teeth, looked in on the boys, then climbed into bed. It was the end of a good run.

# EPILOGUE

In 2005, the Astros took the next step and made it to the World Series for the first time in the history of their franchise. In November 2005, ACTA Sports asked Doug Decatur ten questions about the Houston Astros and their 2005 season.

**AS:** In 2004 you recommended changes to the Astros' batting order in an effort to make the Astros' offense more efficient. Was the same done in 2005?

**DD:** Well, the Astros had three starters in the starting lineup who had never been in a starting lineup before: rookies Willy Taveras and Chris Burke and first-year starter Jason Lane. The Astros also had Morgan Ensberg take on a more important offensive role. Thus, the main focus in 2005 for Phil Garner was to put these guys where they would feel most comfortable and succeed, even if at times that approach was at the expense of a more efficient batting order.

**AS:** You stated in 2004 that, in terms of Win Shares, if all of the Astros' other seven non-pitching positions had the same number of Win Shares as the Astros' catchers had, the 2004 Astros would have only won 51 games. What was done, if anything, about the Astros' catching for the 2005 season?

**DD:** Nothing. Several of the Astros' starting pitchers insisted that the Astros keep Brad Ausmus, and Ausmus bounced back to have his best season in terms of Win Shares since the year 2000. As far as Ausmus' backup goes, the Astros continue to insist that they need a good glove as a backup. Consequently, neither one of the Astros' backup catchers used in 2005 posted an OPS above .475. Conversely, I still contend that the Astros should acquire a backup catcher whose skills better compliment that of starter Brad Ausmus to allow for some type of platooning.

**AS:** Your first recommendation to Phil Garner in 2004 was to recall Brandon Backe. Did you recommend any particular player this season?

**DD:** Phil asked me during the offseason (prior to the 2005 season) to calculate how many games the Astros would win if they started Willy Taveras in center field versus how many games they would win if the Astros signed Jeromy Burnitz and played him in center. The win total came out about even. Thus, I recommended that the Astros go with the younger and cheaper Taveras. So maybe you could argue that I had a little something to do with Taveras starting the year in center.

**AS:** The Astros started the 2005 season with a 15-30 record. What happened?

**DD:** Left field. The Astros decided it wasn't worth it to sign Burnitz to play left field until Berkman returned from the DL and then be stuck with a high priced backup. So the Astros started the season with a hole in left field. For the first 15 games against righthanded pitchers, Phil started Luke Scott. Unfortunately, Scott just wasn't mentally ready to make the jump from AA to the majors. The next 15 games went to Mike Lamb. It was a gamble because there was real concern over Lamb's ability to play left field. Well, the concerns turned out to be justified. Over this 15-game period, the Astros only won three games with Lamb starting in left field. Now I know that I criticized the Reds' GM Dan O'Brien for experimenting with the Reds' shortstops instead of just picking the best one according to the statistics and letting him play. Phil Garner was planning on sticking Scott out there and letting him play until Berkman came back, but Scott just couldn't relax. Lamb was a defensive gamble that quickly showed it wasn't going to work. By this point Phil Garner was ready to drive over to Lance Berkman's house and drag him, bad leg and all, back to the ballpark. Berkman did limp back into the Astros' lineup. But he just wasn't very healthy and hit below .200 for the next 15 games. When the dust settled, the Astros were 15-30 and they were 12^th out of the 13 National League teams in the wild card race.

**AS:** What turned the Astros around in 2005?

**DD**: Berkman got healthy and started hitting like the Lance Berkman we knew. Also Morgan Ensberg started hitting home runs. The Astros were ready to make their 2005 run for the wild card. But was the 15-30 hole too deep? After all, the 1914 Miracle Braves were the only previous team to climb out of a -15 hole. Beginning on May 25, however, with Brandon Backe's victory over the Chicago Cubs, the Astros went 74-43 (.632) for the rest of the season and passed 11 teams in the wild card standings to make the playoffs once again on the final day.

**AS:** What was the one decision that the Astros made during the 2005 season that you disagreed with most?

**DD:** The Astros' management did a fantastic job in 2005. However, if I had to second guess one decision it would be the August 31 decision to send down reliever Mike Burns and recall outfielder Charles Gipson. If you recall, in 2004

I recommended that the Astros go with 11 pitchers for the postseason. By demoting Burns, the Astros had to either go with 10 pitchers in the postseason or put Astacio in their pen. I saw three problems with having Astacio in the pen: (1) Statistically, Burns pitched better in 2005; (2) Burns was a reliever, Astacio wasn't; and (3) Astacio was home run prone. Thus, it would be very dangerous to use Astacio late in a close game. Now, in the Division Series against the Braves, the Astros chose to go with 10 pitchers. In that series, Game 4 went 18 innings, and with only 10 pitchers Roger Clemens had to come in to pitch three innings in relief. Clemens pitched great and I certainly don't want any do-overs, but I don't think Clemens was the same after that game. In Game 3 against the Cardinals in the NLCS, Clemens battled through six innings to get the win, but he only struck out one Cardinal batter. Only once during the regular season did Clemens strike out just one batter in a game. Clemens then broke down in his next start, Game 1 of the World Series. Thus, the argument could be made that not having Burns and, consequently, having to pitch Clemens for three innings of relief in the Division Series, contributed to the Astros losing Game 1 of the World Series. Moreover, after the series against the Braves, the Astros added Astacio to their playoff roster. Burns was not available because of the August 31 roster move. Game 3 of the World Series resulted in another extra inning game. This time in the 14$^{th}$ inning the Astros ran out of pitchers and had to turn to Astacio. Astacio did what he did a lot of in 2005, which was to surrender a home run and ultimately the game. A case could be made that the August 31 demotion of Burns may have contributed to the Astros losing Games 1 and 3 of the World Series. Again, I don't want any do-overs. The Astros did make it to the World Series.

**AS:** So is the reason why the Astros lost the World Series because Mike Burns was demoted?

**DD:** No. But let me give you another reason that you haven't heard anywhere else: DER or Defensive Efficiency Record. DER is the percentage of balls hit in play which a defense turns into outs. *In all seven of the postseason series in 2005, the team in each series with the better regular season DER won that postseason series.* The Astros had the best DER in the NL in 2005, but the White Sox regular season DER was slightly (.005) better. As far as their DERs in the World Series, the White Sox had a great DER of .75. The Astros had a poor World Series DER of just .66.

That is a difference of .09. Based on research from 22 World Series (68-89), 10 times a team had a DER advantage in the World Series of more than .05 and all 10 times the team with the large DER advantage won the Series. Why the .09 difference in the World Series? There are three reasons for fluctuations in DER: (1) good or bad defense; (2) one team hit the ball a lot harder than the other; and (3) luck: one team hit the ball "where-they-ain't" and the other didn't. Over the course of a season, we expect (2) and (3) to even out leaving us with good or bad defense as the difference between DERs of teams. In a short series, however, things may not even out. If the answer was that the White Sox simply hit the ball harder than the Astros we would expect that out of the balls hit in play, the White Sox would have a higher percentage of extra-base hits—and the White Sox did by a slight margin of 9% to 8%. While that's a slight edge, it still doesn't explain the .09 difference in DER. If the difference were due to good or bad defense, then we would expect that in the regular season the White Sox would have had a good DER and the Astros would have had a bad DER, but during the regular season the teams' DERs were practically identical. Thus, this leaves us with only two possibilities: Either in the World Series the White Sox played abnormally good defense, and the Astros played abnormally bad defense and/or the White Sox were abnormally lucky and the Astros were abnormally unlucky. Whatever the case, I blame DER as the main cause for the Astros' World Series defeat. I'll end this DER discussion with a few thoughts: While it was probably somewhat of a coincidence that the winner of each postseason series in 2005 was the team with the better regular season DER, I am certain it wasn't a coincidence that the top three teams in DER in 2005 were the Athletics, White Sox and Astros. These are three teams who understand the importance of good defense. Critics of A's GM Billy Beane say that Beane's *Moneyball* offensive tactics don't really work because the A's aren't really winning with offense. They are winning with pitching. Given the A's 2005 DER information, however, does anyone really think Billy Beane disclosed everything he knows and everything his Athletics do to win in the book *Moneyball*? Could defense also be a big part of his *Moneyball* equation?

**AS:** Roger Clemens had a great season in 2005. Should he have won the Cy Young Award?

**DD:** Yes. Here are the top five pitchers in the NL in 2005 in terms of Win Shares: Roger Clemens (24), Dontrelle Willis (22), Roy Oswalt and Andy Pettitte (21), and Chris Carpenter (20). The AL top 5 were Johan Santana (23), Mark Buehrle (22), Jon Garland (20), Mariano Rivera (19), and Bartolo Colon (18). Carpenter and Colon won the Cy Young Award because they were the only pitchers in their respective leagues to be both in the top five in Win Shares *and* in the top 10 in Run Support. Win Shares can be found in *The Bill James Handbook 2006*.

**AS:** Anything to add on the great 18-inning Division Series game against the Braves?

**DD:** The team with the best "net" wins most games. However, this 18-inning game was the Astros' only postseason game in 2005 where the team with the best "net" didn't win. Net = times on base + total bases + sacrifices - outs used, where a team's times on base = runs + LOB (runners left on base). This means for individual players, non-force out baserunning outs are subtracted from the runner's times on base and double-play groundouts are subtracted from the batter's on base total.

Based on the "nets" the Braves should have won this game 9-5. However, the Astros won 7-6. Ironically, in the last two seasons, there have been only two Astros postseason games where the team with the best "net" didn't win. Both exceptions occurred in Game 4s against the Braves. In 2004, the Braves "stole" game 4. In 2005, the Astros returned the favor.

**AS:** At what point, if any, did you get the feeling that this team was special and that this team might just get to the World Series?

**DD:** At the trading deadline, Phil asked me to research several lefty bats (Adam Dunn, Aubrey Huff, Raul Ibañez, Lyle Overbay, etc.) I did the research and sent the recommendations. The Astros players found out that a deal was in the works and they told Astros management as a group that they didn't want any deals, nor were any deals necessary. They believed that the NL was theirs and management should just sit back and enjoy the ride. It turned out to be one heck of a ride.

# ACKNOWLEDGMENTS

Thanks to the following people who worked on this book:

My lovely wife Caitlin, who did the first edit on the book.

Job Bobbitt, Andy Tollson and Bill Hanks, three friends of mine who were the first to read this book and provided me with valuable feedback.

ACTA Sports, especially John Dewan and Andrew Yankech, for their hard work on this book.

# Cutting-Edge Statistical Resources from ACTA Sports

## THE BILL JAMES HANDBOOK
BILL JAMES and BASEBALL INFO SOLUTIONS

### Available each year on November 1!

Simply put, *The Bill James Handbook* is the best and most complete annual baseball reference guide available today. This book contains a myriad of stats on every hit, pitch and catch in Major League Baseball.

Key features include:

- Pitcher Projections
- Baserunning Analysis
- Hitter Projections
- Career Data for Every Major Leaguer
- Team Efficiency Summary
- Player Win Shares
- Manager's Record

426 pages, paperback, $19.95

## THE HARDBALL TIMES BASEBALL ANNUAL
THE WRITERS OF WWW.HARDBALLTIMES.COM

### Available each year in November!

In this collection of essays and statistical analysis, the entire previous baseball season is broken down from the first pitch to the last out. *The Hardball Times Baseball Annual* even contains a breakdown of the playoffs and World Series. It includes:

- Detailed reviews of how 2005 played out in each of baseball's six divisions.
- Reports on some of the hottest issues in baseball.
- Detailed team stats and graphs.
- Innovative statistics such as Win Shares, line drive/groundball/flyball outcomes.

320 pages, paperback, $17.95

## THE FIELDING BIBLE
JOHN DEWAN and BASEBALL INFO SOLUTIONS

Previously available only to Major League Baseball teams, John Dewan and Baseball Info Solutions reveal their revolutionary approach to fielding analysis. *The Fielding Bible* includes:

- In-Depth Analysis by Position – How do MLB players really stack up against each other defensively? An innovative Plus/Minus System analyzes players position-by-position and provides top-to-bottom rankings and commentary.
- Where Hits Landed – This allows a team to compare their defense point-by-point against other MLB teams.
- Other Special Features – Uniquely designed analysis to determine the best corner infield defenders against the bunt, the best middle infielders on the double play, and the best outfield throwing arms. Plus Bill James' brand new Relative Range Factors and John Dewan's newly designed Zone Ratings!

224 pages, paperback, $19.95

**Available at bookstores or from ACTA Sports • (800) 397-2282 • www.actasports.com**